STRESS
AND
THE POLICE OFFICER

STRESS
AND
THE POLICE OFFICER

By

KATHERINE W. ELLISON, Ph.D.

Department of Psychology
Montclair State College
Upper Montclair, New Jersey

and

JOHN L. GENZ, M.P.A.

Lieutenant
New Jersey State Police
West Trenton, New Jersey

CHARLES C THOMAS • PUBLISHER
Springfield • Illinois • U.S.A.

Published and Distributed Throughout the World by

CHARLES C THOMAS • PUBLISHER
2600 South First Street
Springfield, Illinois 62717

With THOMAS BOOKS *careful attention is given to all details of manufacturing and
design. It is the Publisher's desire to present books that are satisfactory as to their physical
qualities and artistic possibilities and appropriate for their particular use.* THOMAS
BOOKS *will be true to those laws of quality that assure a good name and good will.*

Printed in the United States of America
Q-R-1

Library of Congress Cataloging in Publication Data

Ellison, Katherine W.
    Stress and the police officer.

    Bibliography: p.
    Includes index.
    1. Police — United States — Job Stress. I. Genz,
John L. II. Title.
HV7936.J63E4   1983   363.2'2   83-441
ISBN 0-398-04829-0

In memory of
Barbara Snell Dohrenwend

PREFACE

THE preface is often the most dangerous part of a book. Here authors announce their grand design, couched, perhaps, in terms of the "impossible dream." This is the Achilles' heel on which reviewers can pounce to add new names to the lists of those possessing the tragic flaw of hubris. We had thought at first to cover our backs (to mix metaphors further) by omitting this section; our editor blew our cover.

This book is a collaborative effort in many senses of the word. The senior author (Katherine Ellison) is a social psychologist who began working with police in 1972 as consultant to the New York City Police Department's newly formed Rape Analysis and Investigation Section. At that time, the junior author (John Genz) was an instructor in the New Jersey State Police Academy, charged with setting up a training program on sex crimes investigations. We formed a team, combining academic with practical knowledge.

As we worked together on this project, we realized that the same reactions we were seeing in victims of sexual assault were also common in the officers who worked with them. Perhaps, we reasoned, we should turn our attention to providing support to the professional service deliverer, hoping that as his or her needs were recognized and met, he or she would have a stronger basis for the delicate and difficult task of policing.

We quickly found that the literature on stress in police officers was meager, lacking in a strong theoretical base and in empirical support. Much of it was useless; some was naive to the point of being dangerous. We began to talk with officers, concentrating on those whom others pointed out as people who were doing difficult jobs well with high morale. These interviews, combined with theoretical knowledge about stress gained from Ellison's academic mentor, Professor Barbara Dohrenwend, formed the basis for our article, "The Police Officer as Burned-out Samaritan."

The response to this article included requests to present seminars in stress management. The officers who were our students and team teachers added greatly to our fund of knowledge. With this book we hope to pass on their wisdom, consolidated with knowledge about stress in other occupations and other areas of human endeavor.

We have taken on the difficult task of trying to appeal to several audiences: social scientists interested in occupational stress and students of police science were on our minds, particularly as we wrote the first two chapters, but our first interest was to present the best of current knowledge to police personnel (and those who train them) at all levels of the organization.

We acknowledge here and throughout the book that stress is a complex area. Because it is currently in vogue, research is advancing rapidly, but much remains to be done. Even if the knowledge and technology for stress management were much more advanced, we know how difficult change in organizational patterns or individual behavior can be. Some writers and lecturers offer quick fixes, and outright charlatans have begun to proliferate. We have tried to avoid the trap of simplistic solutions. This makes us humble about the scope of change this effort will produce. How far a book like this can go toward strengthening and supporting good police work we cannot know. For us it is at least partial payment to those who have shared so generously their time and ideas and have convinced us that good policing is possible.

We are, to borrow a phrase from philosopher René Dubos, "despairing optimists." In that spirit, we present *Stress and the Police Officer*.

ACKNOWLEDGMENTS

THIS book is dedicated to the memory of Barbara Snell Dohrenwend, a superb scientist and a gracious and gallant lady. Dr. Dohrenwend was one of the leading researchers in the area of stressful life events; she guided Katherine Ellison's early explorations into the area of stress. Her untimely death was a major life crisis for those of us who had the privilege of knowing and working with her.

Throughout the book we speak of the importance of social support. We also mention the value of giving thanks and praise where it is due. We would now like to practice what we preach and to thank those people whose support and contributions made our work possible.

First, very special thanks go to Robert Buckhout. He encouraged us, searched the literature for pertinent articles, and sent for reprints; he read the manuscript as it evolved, taught us how to work the word processor, and devoted considerable time, energy, and talent to this project. He, particularly, made it possible.

Next, we wish to thank those police officers (and former officers) who contributed to our knowledge of stress in police and showed us that it is possible to do this difficult job well. Officers who have taught stress management courses with us include John Cross, Thomas Granahan, and Joseph Mesmer; also Charles Clark, Rocco Mazza, and Frank Schafer. Some of the others who have shared their expertise with us are Mary Giacchetta, Edward Giblin, Henry Lyons, James Kaljian, Robert Louden, David Smith, James Truhe, Matthew Zaleski, and our colleagues (too numerous to mention) in the New Jersey State Police.

Members of our civilian support network include Eileen Bradley, Rodney George, Judith Mesmer, Alice Read, Thomas Savage, Paul C. Richi, and Florence Weisberg. We are also grateful for the help we received from the library staff of the National Council on Crime and Delinquency, Phyllis Schultze and Sally Kall.

Members of the Genz family who helped with this project are John's parents, Ann Mae and John, his wife, Ann, and his children, Suzanne, Karen, Sharon, and John.

Finally, we acknowledge our debt to our word processor, TRS 80, which saved us countless hours and gave us the luxury of making those little changes which add to clarity and, we hope, elegance in writing.

CONTENTS

STRESS
AND
THE POLICE OFFICER

Chapter 1

THE NATURE OF STRESS

Introduction

EVERYONE agrees that life today can be stressful. So, too, everyone agrees that stress can be harmful; we read of research linking stress with psychological problems, ulcers, heart disease, and a host of other ills (Holmes and Masuda, 1974; Cofer and Appley, 1964; Selye, 1952). Beyond these general statements, there is disagreement among researchers about the specific nature of stress, its effects on physical and psychological well-being, the severity or length of time necessary for a stressful event to lead to damage, and the characteristics of individual biology and personality that may mediate the effects of stressful events. Another area of controversy involves the part played by work situations, family and peer support, cultural expectations, and the like. There is even controversy over the meaning of the term itself.

Finally, because stress is a complex phenomenon, it requires complex research methodology for its study; debate over appropriate approaches rages in the professional literature (Dohrenwend and Dohrenwend, 1974; Coyne and Lazarus, 1979). Also, unfortunately much of the more elegant research has been done in laboratories, under artificial conditions, and may have little applicability to real situations.

Any statements about stress, then, must be made with some caution; no absolute, categorical statements are appropiate, given the current state of knowledge. This does not mean, however, that it is impossible to make a beginning. As in most areas of knowledge, the emphasis is on making educated guesses and on improving percentages.

Another reason for undertaking programs aimed at reducing the potential negative effects of stress before all the returns are in is that virtually all the techniques that have been recommended work to improve the quality of life in other areas as well. Thus, appropriate recognition for good work is thought both to increase efficiency and to decrease the behavior typically associated with stress. Adequate exercise and weight control improve general physical condition, strengthen the heart and lungs, and enhance feelings of well-being while making it easier for the individual to deal with the physical strain put on the body by stressful events.

In stress management, as in almost every other area of human functioning, there is no foolproof formula for success. Individuals differ markedly in the events they define as stressful, in the ways they react to pressure, and in the specific techniques for dealing with stressful events that will be most successful. Despite this, it is possible to offer some suggestions of tactics that work for many people; it is up to each individual to decide how to use this information.

This chapter will present an overview of the research on the nature of stress. The authors do not pretend to be comprehensive in this effort but will concentrate on the most widely held and supported theories.

Definition

A first area of disagreement in stress research is over how the term stress should be used (Dohrenwend and Dohrenwend, 1974; van Dijkuizen, 1980). Some researchers use it to mean the event or situation outside the person, such as extremes of temperature, crowding, physical isolation, loud noise, a new job, shift work, a death in the family, or a reprimand from a superior. Others use it for the inner state of the individual, a state that cannot be measured directly but can be inferred from behavior, such as clenched teeth or expressions of distress, or from some other measurable state, such as the level of certain chemicals in the blood. Anxiety, anger, joy, frustration, sadness fit into this category. (Indeed, Cofer and Appley [1964] point out rather irritably that "it has all but preempted a field previously shared by a number of other concepts," [p.441] including frustration, conflict, and anxiety. They and others seem to feel that such a broad scope so dilutes the meaning of the term as to make it almost meaningless, and certainly makes it virtually impossible to study with any scientific rigor.)

A third common use of the term stress is in referring to an observable response to an external (or internal) stimulus or situation, a response such as sweating palms, pounding heart, yelling and cursing, increased adrenaline flow, and the like. To attempt to clear up some of this confusion, some researchers suggest the use of the terms stressors, or stressful events, for the stimulus and strain for the response.

The psychologist Richard Lazarus (1966) points out that while both the environmental stimulus and the reacting individual are vital elements, it is the nature of the interaction — the relationship between the two — that is crucial. He defines stress as "a very broad class of problems differentiated from other problem areas because it deals with any demands which tax the system, . . . and the response of that system." The present authors find this broad definition the most useful one. In the interest of clarity, this book will use the terms stressors, stressful events, or pressures to refer to the stimulus, or cause, the term stress reaction for the response, and the general term stress for the entire process.

Stress and Coping

According to the definition, any demand placed on the person or any event that is experienced by the individual as change (and the individual's definition of the situation is very important) is stressful to some degree; however, not all change, or even all change perceived as harmful, necessarily leads to negative consequences. Most people do not become severely disabled physically or psychologically when terrible things happen to them, and those who do become disabled often regain their equilibrium in a reasonably short time (Hudgens, 1974). A study of the effects of stressful life events by Chiriboga and Cutler (1979) even found that negative stress was associated with improved psychosocial functioning in approximately one-third of their cases. Similarly, Antonovsky (1971) found that more than 25 percent of concentration camp survivors, studied twenty-five years after their release, showed no evidence of psychiatric disorder or chronic physical disease.

Indeed, some change — some arousal — seems to be necessary for people to function well. The relationship between ability to cope and adapt and amount of stress usually is described as an "inverted U" shaped function (Monat and Lazarus, 1977); that is, people function best when arousal is at a moderate level (as they define moderate) and poorly when arousal is either very high or very low. At the extremes, people who are subjected to severe sensory deprivation, as in solitary confinement or some forms of brainwashing (and certain psychological experiments designed to test the phenomenon), describe the experience as extremely stressful and often suffer from hallucinations, which become more vivid, complex, and intense with time (Heron, 1961).[1]

Change (and the stress reactions it may bring) has another important function. Under pressure, the person searches for ways to cope and may find new behaviors that help him adapt to changing conditions. Coping, in fact, has been defined as "adaptation under relatively difficult conditions" (White, 1974).

Complicating this picture is the evidence that individuals differ in the extent to which they seek or avoid change. Hans Selye, often called the father of stress research, asserts (rather simplistically, perhaps) that "there are two main types of human beings: 'racehorses,' who thrive on stress, and are only happy with a vigorous, fast-paced lifestyle; and 'turtles,' who in order to be happy require peace, quiet, and a generally tranquil environment — something that would frustrate and bore most racehorse types" (1978, p. 60).[2] For example, some police officers join the force because they are looking for challenge, excitement, and adventure (Walsh, 1977); they thrive in situations in which things are happening constantly. They would be miserable and probably inefficient doing laboratory work or identifying fingerprints. Others join because they want security; they may work best in assignments involving well-ordered routine (Walsh, 1977) and be rattled and inefficient in a job such as undercover narcotics investigation.

Since some pressure is helpful, what are the conditions under which stress can lead to physical and psychological damage? There is no simple answer, but important factors include the intensity of the stressor, the length of its duration, its meaning for the individual, the kind of coping skills he has developed, and the reaction of others to the stressful event or situation and to the individual. To generalize, it is when one is confronted with too many stressful events, or too severe ones, in too short a period of time, or for too extended a period of time with too few personal, organizational, or social supports that stress can lead to trouble.

Individual Personality Factors

"He's strong; he can take anything." "He goes to pieces over the least little problem." Comments of this sort spotlight the common belief that there are individual differences in ability to cope; indeed, the commonsense view seems to be that individual personality factors are the only variables worthy of consideration in understanding stress reactions. Although social scientists do consider other variables, as will be discussed later, they have expended much time and energy on research into traits, personality types, and styles of thinking that seem to influence the way individuals deal with conflict, frustration, and change in general.

By far the best known of the theories linking personality style to stress reactions, and then to disease, has been Friedman and Rosenman's (1974) work on the link between heart disease and a behavior pattern that they have called "Type A." The type A person is aggressive, competitive, and hostile. He feels as if he is always "under the gun"; there never seems to be enough time, and the pressure to achieve weighs heavily upon him. Type A men are reported to be seven times more likely to develop coronary disease than the more easygoing type B. These people may be quite as ambitious and successful as the type A's, but they are slower to anger, feel less rushed and impatient, and are generally more tolerant of others and of themselves. Exactly how this pressurized life-style leads to disease is unclear, although they hypothesize that it may be related to increased amounts of the hormones adrenaline and noradrenaline in the blood (Monat and Lazarus, 1977).

The work of Friedman and Rosenman has generated a spate of other studies which have tended to confirm it (Jenkins, 1976). One such study followed over 3,000 men for eight years. Men who exhibited type A behavior at the beginning of the study showed twice the rate of new coronary heart disease and were five times more likely to have a second myocardial infarction during the follow-up period than men not exhibiting type A behavior. This effect could not be explained by the influence of other factors such as blood pressure and cigarette smoking (Holroyd, 1979). Glass (1977) concludes that this behavior pattern can be understood as a "characteristic style of responding to environmental stress which is appraised as a threat to the individual's sense of control" (p. 104).

Critics of Friedman and Rosenman (Innes, 1981) doubt that people can be so easily divided into two distinct, discontinuous types. It is much more likely, they feel, that people fall along a continuum: that most people are somewhere in the middle and have characteristics of both type A and type B. They further point out that a statistical relationship between two variables does not necessarily mean that one causes the other (or, as statisticians would say, correlation does not imply causation).

Another characteristic that may determine reactions to external events is what Kobasa (1979) has called "hardiness." She believes that "stress-resistant people have a specific set of attitudes toward life — an openness to change, a feeling of involvement in whatever they are doing, and a sense of control over events. . . .they score high on 'challenge' (viewing change as a challenge rather than a threat), 'commitment' (the opposite of alienation), and 'control' (the opposite of powerlessness)" (Pines, 1980, pp. 34, 36). She has found differences in health to be related to these factors.

The fit between the needs and style of the person and the environment also influences whether a situation will be stressful for an individual. It is not the individual's personality type per se or the situation per se that is maladaptive; the key to whether the individual thrives may lie, in a given environment, in the appropriateness of his needs and behavioral style for that situation. An example of this may be found in the literature on leadership. An authoritarian leader, one who gives orders and expects them to be obeyed instantly, without question, is most appropriate in a riot. In that setting it would be disastrous to poll the group members for their opinions: "Joe, do you think we should move in? Elliot, what's your view?" Usually, however, such a leader does not obtain good results over an extended period, particularly with followers accustomed to a more democratic style. In everyday situations, the democratic leader, who encourages participation from his men, increases their commitment to the goals of the organization and gets better performance. Morale tends to be higher in groups with democratic leaders (Hampton, Summer, and Webber, 1978; Iannone, 1980).

The fit between person and environment can also be seen in a somewhat different way. In addition to the fit between the individual and his objective situation, there is the matter of the fit between the situation and the individual's perception of it. This is the variable Lazarus (1966) calls "cognitive appraisal." This view holds that an important, perhaps crucial, element in whether or not any given event or situation produces stress reactions and physical and/or psychological problems in an individual is that person's thoughts and beliefs about it. For example, for one person a new job or assignment might be seen as a challenge, an opportunity to show what he can do. For another, it might be a threat, seen only as another opportunity to fail or make a fool of himself. Obviously the new job would be more stressful for the second person than for the first. Indeed, severel currently popular styles of psychotherapy, including rational emotive therapy (Ellis, 1975) and cognitive behavior modification (Meichenbaum, 1977), are based on the belief that psychological problems result from distorted, irrational ways of thinking. (These ways of thinking will be considered in detail in a later chapter.)

Certain areas of belief have particular impact on the way people handle potentially stressful situations. One of these is the perception that people can control what happens to them. Some people seem to believe that they are largely responsible for what happens to them, while others believe their lives are primarily controlled by luck, fate, or other forces outside themselves. Psychologist Julian Rotter (1966) has called these beliefs about the part we play in our own lives "locus of control." Those people who believe they control their own destinies are said to have a high degree of internal locus of control, while the tendency to hold others responsible is external locus of control.

People with internal locus of control have been shown to have less debilitating anxiety than externals (Strassberg, 1973). They are more content with life (Naditch, Gargan, and Michael, 1975), less likely to be depressed (Lefcourt, 1976; Strickland, 1974), and less suicidal (Strickland, 1977). They exercise more (Walker, 1973), are less likely to smoke (Coan, 1973), and suffer less hypertension (Naditch, 1974) and coronary disease (Cromwell et al., 1977).[+]

A belief that people can control what happens to them lessens stress reactions, even when events are unpleasant or noxious. Subjects in one experiment were told that they would receive six moderately strong electric shocks within the space of a half hour. Half of the subjects were told that they could control when the shocks occurred; the others were told that they could not influence the timing in any way. The first group had significantly weaker physiological responses following the shocks than did the second group and reported being less upset. It was even found that those subjects who could not control the shock were better off if they at least knew when to expect it. If the experimenter gave the subject a signal, such as a bell, a few seconds before the onset of shock, the subjects showed fewer stress reactions than those who had no warning (Staub et al., 1971). (Interestingly, the same phenomenon has been found in rats [Weiss, 1971].) Predictability, then, is another factor that lessens the potential negative effects of change.

Many police officers the authors have observed find that they can most effectively control what happens in an encounter with citizens if they give the suspect or victim the perception that he can determine how it is to happen. When making an arrest, the officer may say, "You are under arrest, and you are going to jail. You can go one of two ways: you can make a fool of yourself in front of your family, or you can walk out with dignity."

The relationship of locus of control to stress reactions is not as simple as it seems, however. Although it is good to believe that a person can control his own destiny, in reality the person may have no power to control; therefore, he may frequently find himself confronted with experiences that belie his beliefs. This experience of "constantly butting one's head up against a stone wall" often leads to the phenomenon of "learned helplessness."

Just as people (and animals) can learn to get reward and avoid punishment — the processes known as conditioning — so, too, can they learn that they have no power to influence their own fates. When they are exposed over a period of time to situations in which rewards and/or punishments are delivered capriciously, they give up trying and become apathetic and depressed (Seligman, 1975). For example, battered wives who stay in their marriages may be reacting out of learned helplessness. Because of the capriciousness of the battering, they come to believe that nothing they can do will make any difference and that their only recourse is to accept their fate. Once a person learns that he is helpless, a change in the objective situation may be insufficient to induce him to try again. He must almost be dragged through coping experiences to learn that his behavior can make a difference.

Even if one cannot control a potentially stressful event, problems are lessened if it is predictable. Laboratory research has shown, for example, that people report less severe physical symptoms during predictable bursts of noise than during unpredictable ones (Weidner and Matthews, 1978). Until recently, pediatricians believed that it was best not to tell children who were to be hospitalized for surgery anything about the experience beforehand; they reasoned that if they knew about the discomfort, they would be difficult to handle before the operation. Current experience contradicts this belief. Now children are often given a run-through of the experience and warned to expect pain. Those children who have this preparation seem to have fewer physical and psychological complications from the hospital stay (Meichenbaum, Turk, and Burstein, 1975).[5]

Another nuance in moderating the deleterious effects of pressure involves understanding what is happening and why. This is particularly true if the individual can get a sense of meaning and purpose for a stressful incident.

> **Case 1:1.** The sheriffs of two large, neigboring counties were faced with serious problems of overcrowding in the jails. Both were ordered to canvas other jails in the state and find places to transfer prisoners. Sheriff A was told to transfer forty prisoners, while Sheriff B had six to move. Both found a jail that had room for their prisoners, but it was over 500 miles away.
>
> Sheriff B sent his six prisoners off routinely. Sheriff A made personal calls to the next of kin of each of the prisoners he was to transfer. The conversation went something like this:
>
> *Sheriff:* This is Sheriff Finnerty.[6]
>
> *Kin:* Are you really the sheriff? (or similar expressions of surprise and disbelief).

S: (After assurances of his identity) I'm afraid I have some bad news for you. I've had to transfer your son (husband, etc.) to the jail in (Jailtown), and that is 500 miles away.

K: (A variety of expletives, which the sheriff claims added greatly to his vocabulary and which he allowed the person to get off his/her chest.)

S: Let me try to explain this to you. I know this is an inconvenience to you, but I'd rather be calling you with this news, than to have to call you to say that your son had died in a fire in an overcrowded jail.

Sheriff B found himself with six lawsuits on his hands; Sheriff A had none.

People, and events that put pressure on them, are, of course, embedded in a social context, and the response of people who are important to us influences the way we will deal with pressure (Innes, 1981; Cobb, 1976). Simply having other people around, of course, is not enough; the nature of the interaction can exacerbate or alleviate potential pressure (Innes, 1981). The nature of the response is important; calm in those around us tends to beget calm in us (Epley, 1974; Rachman, 1978), and feeling responsible for others who are under pressure as well may increase one's own tension (Innes, 1981).

Case 1:2. The wife of a prominent mental health professional was raped and beaten in the women's restroom of a public building. She waited several days to tell her husband about the incident. He questioned her sharply about it, probing for details and berating her and himself. Several days later he told her that he had recounted her story to his own therapy group and that it was their opinion that she had not been raped at all, that, instead, she had been with a lover, and had needed a plausible excuse for bruises he gave her. A year later this woman still suffers from severe headaches, depression, and crying spells, which professional help has failed to change. One of her adolescent daughters also has major problems.[7]

Of course, the responses of everyone in the social support network are not equally powerful. The response of authority figures to whom one looks for guidance in defining the situation may be particularly potent (Bard and Ellison, 1974). Victims of violent crimes (particularly sexual assaults) have sometimes reported that the impact of the crime itself was mild compared to the trauma of insensitive behavior by health and criminal justice professionals (Brodyaga et al., 1975; Holstrom and Burgess, 1978).

Support may also be insufficient when the stressor continues unabated. LaRocco and Jones, in a study of Navy personnel, found that support, whether from one's leader or peers, did not appear to be an effective means of removing the negative influences of stress produced by conflict and ambiguity (undated).

Finally, coping style must be considered. Mechanic (1962) has argued that there are two kinds of reactions to stressful events: task-oriented, in which the individual concentrates on the situation and strategies for dealing with it (strategies often known as problem solving), and defense oriented, concerned with protecting the ego from hurt and disruption. Task-oriented strategies involve defining the problem, seeking and evaluating options, deciding what to do, doing it, and getting and evaluating feedback. The appropriate solution may be to attack the problem directly, to retreat, or to compromise. Defensive behavior patterns tend to deny or distort reality. These are the behaviors which the abnormal psychology books refer to as "defense mechanisms" (Coleman, Butcher, and Carson, 1980).

Some professionals who specialize in behavior problems believe that refusing to face the truth is always self-defeating. Lazarus (1979) disagrees, giving evidence that denial is appropriate when the person has no control over the situation. Problem solving may also fail when there is inadequate information on which to base a sound judgment.

Furthermore, the strategy that may work in one situation or at one time in a person's life may not succeed in others. Chodoff and his colleagues (1964) found that parents of children dying of leukemia were helped by avoidance and denial defenses before the child's death but suffered more afterwards. Observers of mental health professionals often note with some bemusement that people who are superb in helping others deal with problems may be inadequate to solve their own. While total competence and flexibility may be a goal toward which to strive, it is "an ideal probably no one achieves" (Lazarus, 1979, p. 60).

Stressful Life Events

It goes without saying that events differ in the strain they put on abilities to adapt. Studies of the relative stressfulness of a variety of events and of the possibility that stressors may add up to create problems have occupied much of the recent literature on stress. The current wave of interest in stressful life events received its impetus from the work of psychiatrist Thomas Holmes and his colleagues (Holmes and Holmes, 1970; Holmes and Rahe, 1967; Holmes and Masuda, 1974). They asked people from several countries to rate how stressful each of a number of commonly experienced events was, on a scale of 0 to 100. They took the average value for each item, and came up with a scale reproduced in Chapter 3 (see Table 3-I).

Using this scale, the researchers asked people to check off the events that they had experienced. They also asked them to answer questions designed to measure their physical and emotional health. They found that people who had experienced changes that totalled more than 300 "life change units" (LCU) within one year had a much greater risk of serious physical or emotional problems within the next two years than did people who had experienced fewer changes. In one group of eighty-four subjects, illness was reported by 49 percent of the high-risk group (300 plus LCU), 25 percent of the medium-risk group (200 to 299 LCU), and 9 percent of those at low risk (150 to 190 LCU) (Holmes and Masuda, 1974).

The reader who has added up his own LCU and is contemplating increasing his insurance can take heart from the flood of criticism that followed the publication of these findings. Many subsequent studies have failed to find such a clear-cut relationship between number of events and illness (Goldberg and Comstock, 1976). Some researchers have also questioned the logic of combining positive and negative stressors (Johnson and Sarason, 1979) and have developed scales that allow individuals to say for themselves how great the impact upon them of various events had been (Sarason, Johnson, and Siegel, 1978; Sarason, 1981). The events, in addition, are not completely independent of each other. A divorce generally carries with it some of the elements lower on the scale: change in social activities, revision of personal habits, and the like.

The possibility is also strong that the cause-and-effect relationship implied by much of the work on stressful life events is not so direct as it might seem, that many other factors interact with these events (Jenkins, 1979). Simply to count events ignores the anxiety of anticipation, chronic stress, and wished-for events that do not happen. Any conclusions about stressful life events, then, must be tentative (Dohrenwend and Dohrenwend, 1974). Certainly a high score is not a signal to suspend all activity. At most, it might serve the concerned individual as cause for reflection and perhaps a reconsideration of the factors described in the preceding section that may moderate the potential harmful consequences of these events and of the specific suggestions that will be given later for stress reduction.

Influence of Organizational Factors

Those people who argue that individual factors alone are sufficient to explain stress reactions and, consequently, that all attempts at modifying these reactions should focus on individuals ignore much of the research of social and organizational psychology. Common sense and research findings tell us that some occupations are more stressful than others. The air traffic controller at a busy facility such as New York's Kennedy or Chicago's O'Hare Airport is under more external stress than is the college professor at a busy facility such as Ohio State University or the City University of New York. Cobb (1978) found hypertension was four times as high among air traffic controllers as among pilots, with diabetes and peptic ulcers more than twice as high. Furthermore, the busier the airport, the higher the rate of these conditions.

Stressfulness of a job may differ with one's position in the hierarchy. In general, the more control one has over one's working conditions, the less pressure one feels. A study of over 2,000 Canadians working in a large bureaucratic organization found that managers showed fewer stress reactions than did staff and operations people (Zaleznik, Kets de Vries, and Howard, 1977). This difference seemed to be related to high accountability, red tape, uncertain lack of coordination, and ambivalence about leadership and performance evaluation among the staff and operations groups.

A review of the literature on occupational stress yields five categories of factors in the work environment that can act as stressors: (1) factors intrinsic to the job, (2) role in the organization, (3) relationships within the organization, (4) career development, and (5) organizational structure and climate (Cooper and Marshall, 1977).

Factors intrinsic to the job that may be stressful include poor physical working conditions, the pressures of decision making, and a dehumanizing atmosphere, such as is found on the paced assembly line. Shifts that rotate on a weekly or monthly basis also are frequently mentioned as a pressure that decreases efficiency and can seriously affect health (Folkard and Monk, 1979; Meers, Maasen, and Verhaagen, 1978).

Much research shows that role expectations play an important part in determining behavior in all aspects of life. In industrial settings, for example, it is common to see a staunch supporter of the rights of workers become, upon promotion to supervisor, a staunch advocate of company policy. Many of us have had the experience of returning to our parents' home after years of living on our own to find that they still think of us as children and expect to be able to dictate our behavior accordingly.

A powerful demonstration of the importance of role expectations was provided by psychologist Philip Zimbardo (Zimbardo, 1973). Zimbardo recruited twenty-one young men to participate in research on the effects of imprisonment. All were normal and healthy on psychological tests. A mock prison was set up, and half of the subjects were assigned to be guards, while the other half were prisoners. Within a few days, the guards were acting in abusive, dehumanizing ways toward the prisoners, and the prisoners became demoralized and turned against one another. Some became so upset and their behavior so bizarre that it was necessary to release them. The demonstration, scheduled to last for two weeks was stopped after a few days.

Other studies with American prisoners of war in the Korean conflict showed no personality differences between the 85 percent who cooperated with their Chinese captors and the 15 percent who did not (Naughton, 1975). Closer to home, criminologist George Kirkham describes the changes in attitude he experienced when he went from being a college professor to police officer. Not only were his attitudes about policing changed, but he also found himself behaving in ways he had formerly condemned (Kirkham, 1974).

Two major organizational factors frequently mentioned as stressful have to do with the role one is expected to take in the organization, role ambiguity and role conflict. Role ambiguity involves "a lack of clarity about the work objectives associated with the role, about colleagues' expectations of the work role and about the scope and responsibilities of the job" (Cooper and Marshall, 1977, p. 24). The person does not know what is expected of him, what behavior will bring reward or punishment. Role ambiguity is sometimes heightened by discrepancies between the official job description and the reality of the work one is asked to do.

Role conflict comes when the worker is torn between conflicting job demands, particularly demands from two groups of people who expect different kinds of behavior. Thus, the lieutenant may have one standard for a patrol officer's behavior, while fellow patrolmen have quite another (and the mayor and press another still). Such incompatibility of job demands tends to be especially high in positions where the job holders have the responsibility for dealing simultaneously with some people inside the organization and some outside it (Kahn, 1978): of trying, for example, to establish rapport with a potential informant while being pressured to "keep up the numbers" by a supervisor.

One of the most frequent forms of role conflict is work overload. It is as if the worker is saying, "I don't object to the things I am asked to do, and I don't find them unreasonable, but I can't meet all the demands at once" (Kahn, 1978). Overload has been associated with cardiovascular disease, escapist drinking, absenteeism, low motivation, lowered self-esteem, and unwillingness to make suggestions to employers (Margolis, Kroes, and Quinn, 1974). A somewhat different form of work overload comes when the job is too difficult (Kahn, 1978).

Just as too much to do can lead to problems, so can too little: the work underload that leads to boredom. The impact of underload or overload may vary from job to job. One study found that underload seems to have little effect on the job dissatisfaction of assembly line workers and police officers but increases dissatisfaction for scientists. The relationship for administrators is unclear (Harrison, 1975). Others (Kroes, 1976) disagree and consider underload an important stressor for police.

A final factor related to role is responsibility. Although in general the job of the manager is less stressful than that of workers at the bottom of the organizational ladder (probably in part because of their greater control over their conditions of work), at least one study has found that people who are responsible for other people have higher blood pressure and serum cholesterol levels and are heavier smokers than people who are responsible for things (Coan, 1973).[8]

Stress at work also comes from poor relationships with superiors, colleagues, and subordinates. Of course, liking the people with whom one works does not, in itself, ensure efficiency. In the work setting, many would prefer a colleague, subordinate, or boss who, though lacking in social graces, was competent to a pleasant, friendly incompetent. This is especially so if our efficiency depends in part on his. Still, few of us do our best for a boss who is personally abusive or with subordinates who dislikes us. While some managers denigrate the importance of good relations with subordinates — "I don't want them to like me, I just want them to do the work" — unhappy subordinates can, and often do, turn their constructive energies to sabotage (Hampton, Summer, and Webber, 1980).

Lack of opportunities for career development include lack of job security and, for the ambitious, inability to advance as far and as fast as they feel capable. It is a particular problem in times of economic hardship that people who had come on a job expecting, quite reasonably, a bright future with many promotions are thwarted later in their careers by tightened budgets. Overpromotion, which happens in some civil service jobs where advancement is based on ability to take tests that may be only marginally related to job performance, also can create problems. There is no assurance that ability to do well on multiple choice tests is related to ability to work with people. This is part of the problem posed by the famous satirical essay *The Peter Principle* (Peter, 1969).

A final factor, one that has received much attention in the organizational psychology literature, is organizational structure and climate. It has been found that participation by workers in the decision-making process of the organization increases productivity and job satisfaction and decreases turnover (Schultz, 1982; Hampton, Summer, and Webber, 1980). This is related, again, to the need to feel some control over one's life.

Desirable conditions of work, then, seem to be —

1. work that is mentally challenging (within the limits of the worker's abilities) and interesting;
2. work that is not physically exhausting;
3. rewards that are just, are in line with the person's expectations, and include knowledge of reasons for the reward;
4. pleasant working environment;
5. work of which one can be proud;
6. support from supervisors, co-workers, and subordinates (Locke, 1976).

Although there is extensive evidence to support the differing effects of work conditions, the correlations are, at best, modest, and the effects on job satisfaction, mental and physical health, and productivity moderate (Kasl, 1978). The same, of course, is true for most epidemiological research, such as the evidence of the effects of smoking on lung cancer: while risk is greatly increased, most people who smoke do not develop the disease.

Institutional Dehumanization — Burnout

The notion of burnout has captured the public's imagination to the extent that it has become an almost fashionable condition (Morrow, 1981). Malaise of every description may now be attributed to its pernicious effects; we hear of it among students, photographers, housewives, athletes, and executives. It has even been blamed for the elusiveness of the artist's muse. As with the general notion of stress, the definition of burnout has been extended so broadly as to be almost meaningless (especially as an area for research). Furthermore, although it lacked the catchy title, the phenomenon itself was described long before Freundenberger so christened it in the mid-1970s, in work such as Niederhoffer's *Behind the Shield* (1969).

To narrow this focus, the authors find it most useful to follow Maslach's (1976) lead and confine use of the term to a special reaction to chronic job stress found in people whose jobs involve a great deal of contact with the public. This contact is in roles that involve the interpersonal management tasks found in human service delivery jobs, especially in what have been called the helping professions. As does Maslach, the authors prefer to emphasize the part played by the organization and to use as a synonym the term institutional dehumanization.

In this definition, burnout is the tendency to cope with stress by a form of distancing, which not only hurts the professional but also is damaging to his ability to serve the public (Maslach, 1976; Cherniss, 1980). Distancing, of course, is a matter of degree. Some distancing — objectivity — is necessary to allow one to work in situations that bring one in constant contact with human misery. How, then, is burnout different from these normal defenses which facilitate competence or from other indications of job dissatisfaction such as turnover or temporary fatigue?

Maslach describes a variety of symptoms that point to a person who is burning out. The idealism, enthusiasm, and hope that characterize many entrants into the human service professions are lost (Cherniss, 1980). The professional becomes cynical and develops negative feelings about his clients. He may begin to speak of them as less than human. (The television program "Hill Street Blues" has added a number of particularly colorful derogatory terms to police vocabulary, especially "dog breath.") The person who is burning out withdraws from contact with clients and may barricade himself behind desk or clipboard and avoid eye contact. The mirrored sunglasses favored by some police officers serve this function.

Withdrawal is further characterized by sharp distinctions between job and personal life. The person who has burned out refuses to discuss work with his spouse. At the extreme, pictures of family come down from desk or locker, as if even this contact would sully his personal life. Another form of withdrawal is through intellectualization and the use of precise professional jargon. Surgeons speak of patients as "the kidney," psychiatric nurses of "the obsessive-compulsive," and lawyers of "the docket" (Cherniss, 1980).

Other behaviors taken as symptoms of burnout include apathy, decline in motivation, effort, and involvement with work, frequent irritability and anger with clients and colleagues, preoccupation with one's own comfort and welfare on the job, tendency to rationalize failure by blaming the clients or the system, and resistance to change, growing rigidity, and loss of creativity (Cherniss, 1980). It is the "transformation of a person with original thought and creativity on the job into a mechanical bureaucrat (Maslach, 1976), one who goes strictly by the book rather than by the unique circumstances of each situation (Ellison and Genz, 1978).

Maslach (1976), in a study of more than 200 social welfare workers, psychiatric nurses, poverty lawyers, prison personnel, and child care workers, reported that "the majority" showed symptoms of burnout. While this study is much cited, it is long on generalized conclusions and short on data. Further work with seventy-six staff members from mental health institutions is somewhat more specific (Pines and Maslach, 1978). Variables found to correlate with negative attitudes toward the job and toward patients included long hours with seriously disturbed patients, frequent staff meetings, constant contact with patients (as opposed to inability to withdraw and do other work from time to time), and working alone, as opposed to sharing the load with other professionals. Expectations also played a part. Staff members with graduate degrees were more likely to enter the work with high expectations of clients and themselves and to become more cynical than those with less education and lower expectations. The longer professionals had been in mental health work, the less they liked the work, the clients, and themselves.

In a longitudinal study of twenty-eight new professionals in the human service occupations of high school teaching, public service law, public health nursing, and mental health work, Cherniss (1980) found the symptoms of burnout in 75 percent after only eighteen months. He laid the bulk of the blame on factors outside the individual, such as lack of realistic training, lack of support from the organization and from colleagues, and cultural developments — professional mystique and the unrealistic expectations it has fostered — calling burnout a "reflection of institutional deficit or weakness" and concluding that "any attempt to identify professional burnout as the individual professional's 'problem' and to deal with it accordingly will be misguided and ultimately ineffective" (p. 217).

Writers on the subject differ in their assessment of the importance of individual personality styles on burnout. Freundenberger (1974), arguing for their impact, suggests that three personality types are prone to burnout. The dedicated worker is committed but takes on too much work too intensely, subjecting himself to overload. The outside life of the overcommitted worker is unsatisfactory, and he puts all his emotional eggs in the basket of the job. The authoritarian so needs control he believes no one else can do the job as well as he. Cherniss (1980) and Kahn (1978) also argue that burnout is particularly prevalent in those who were initially dedicated and enthusiastic and, perhaps, held unrealistic expectations of their ability to help others. Kahn remarks that "some people never burn out because they were never on fire to begin with." Research from social psychology also shows that people who are particularly trusting initially become particularly cynical when that trust is abused, while those who expected less of others to begin with had more positive attitudes toward others in the long run (Cummings et al., 1971).

Both Maslach and Cherniss believe that, although burnout is not inevitable, once it has occurred it may be irreversible. The worker who has burned out might seriously consider moving on to another assignment or another career.

While descriptive evidence for burnout abounds, as do hypotheses about it, hard evidence about the conditions that foster burnout, its course over time, and its relative prevalence in various occupational groups is largely lacking. Most of the research does not study workers over time but relies on cross-sectional evidence, and most is correlational. Fortunately, the suggestions that have been made for preventing burnout are similar to recommendations organizational psychologists make for increasing job satisfaction and efficiency.

Influence of Other Environmental Factors

Conditions in the environment that act as stressors are varied. In addition to the stressful life events that Holmes and his colleagues studied, there are accidental events such as fires, floods, earthquakes, and similar "acts of God," crime victimization, sudden accidents, and sudden illnesses: events that are sudden, unpredictable, and, from the victim's viewpoint, arbitrary.

Although most people who experience such trauma eventually recover (Weil, 1973), in most there is at least some short-term disruption. (This will be covered in greater depth in the section on crisis reactions.) One estimate states that approximately one-third of the survivors of natural disasters may display a "disaster syndrome," appearing dazed, wandering around aimlessly, and complaining of severe physical symptoms such as nausea, insomnia, and "shakiness" (Smith, Sarason, and Sarason, 1982).

Some studies of disaster victims show more severe consequences.

Ahearn (1981) reported increased numbers of requests for psychiatric help lasting for three years after a major earthquake in Nicaragua, and studies of a flood in Buffalo Creek, West Virginia, which killed 125 people and left 4,000 homeless, showed more than 80 percent of the survivors suffered severe psychological problems more than three years after the disaster (Erikson, 1976; Lifton and Olson, 1976; Titchener and Kapp, 1976; Glesner, Green, and Winget, 1978).

Reaction to disaster is influenced by its intensity, scope, and duration, by community morale, by fears about its recurrence, and by long-term consequences. Feelings of inability to find meaning in what happened and a belief that an uncaring outsider caused the damage — and could be expected to act with similar disregard for one's future needs — were particularly likely to be associated with severe, long-range problems (Erikson, 1976; Silver and Wortman, 1980).

More chronic conditions in the environment also take their toll. Needless to say, living with the constant threat of war, as people in Northern Ireland and parts of the Middle East have, may lead to major changes in personality (Fields, 1976). The effects of combat have also been amply documented (Coleman, Butcher, and Carson, 1980), both the short-lived "combat neurosis" and the post-trauma stress syndrome are now being described in Viet Nam veterans ten years after their combat experience.

Closer to home, poverty certainly is a stressor, as is living in a neighborhood where crime, decay, and filth are prevalent and chronic. Unemployment has been associated with increases in depression and in violence, particularly family violence (Nelson, 1974; Brenner, 1973).

A stressor that may interact with those discussed previously is living in a family that is chaotic, or even simply disorganized, or in which one or more members have severe problems such as alcohol or drug dependence, psychosis or severe neurosis, or criminal activity. Stress in these situations often involves a vicious circle or, more accurately, a downward spiral. Conflicts of individual personalities or needs lead to fighting or other disruption. The stress reactions produced by this disruption in turn affect the individual's work, which increases the stress and leads to more fights at home (Handy, 1978). By the same token, a happy family life can buffer the effects of a high-pressure job.

Influence of Sociocultural Factors

Perception of a situation as stressful or challenging is not entirely the result of factors in an individual's personality. Societies and cultures play a large part in defining success and failure and in setting role expectations. Fear of aging, for example, is not the problem in a culture that respects and rewards the wisdom of age that it is in a culture such as ours, where old is seen as ugly and the elderly as a burden (Townsend, 1957). Similarly, the death of a child is much more stressful in a society such as ours, which puts a high emotional value on children and childhood (and has a low infant mortality rate) than it was in sixteenth century Europe, where half of all children could be expected to die before the age of six and in which children were a severe economic burden in a marginal economy (Aries, 1962).

Universal Stressors

Situations that are life threatening, that involve a constant struggle to obtain the necessities of life — food, shelter, and the like — or that involve continuous physical discomfort, such as extremes of temperature or chronic pain, are universally stressful (to animals as well as humans). Similar events that evoke at least temporary stress reactions in everyone are stimulus overload, such as that found in combat, and stimulus deprivation.

Human beings are social animals. Cataclysmic destruction of community, as happened in Hiroshima and Nagasaki, and in Buffalo Creek, West Virginia (with the flood described earlier), is stressful not only because it is life threatening but also because it deprives people of a supportive group who can help in recovery (Erikson, 1976; Lifton, 1968). The importance of a supportive group has been described also in studies of prisoners of war. Prisoners confined with others fared far better, physically and psychologically, than those in solitary confinement (Naughton, 1975). Fortunately, most of us, in our society, seldom encounter such situations, and when we do encounter them, our exposure is short.

Physical Responses to Stressful Events

When a person or animal perceives danger, the body responds in ways that prepare it to cope. There are "major outpourings of powerful hormones creating dramatic alterations in bodily processes many of which we sense in the case of a pounding heart, sweating, trembling, fatigue, etc." (Monat and Lazarus, 1976). The classic, and for many years unchallenged, work on the physiological reactions to stressors is Hans Selye's (1956) description of a general adaptation syndrome (GAS). Selye believes that the body responds to any demands on it in ways that are similar, regardless of the nature of the demand. The pinch hitter sent in at a crucial moment of the game has the same kind of physical reactions (if not of the same intensity or duration) as the soldier going into combat at the front line.

The GAS has three stages: shock and alarm, resistance, and exhaustion. The first stage has the physiological changes usually associated with emotions: the heart pounds, hands and feet sweat, pupils of the eyes dilate. In addition to these noticeable reactions, the blood pressure first falls then rises sharply. The hormone adrenaline (epinephrine) flows. In some cases, strength increases greatly, giving the phenomenon beloved of newspapers that finds a 115-pound woman lifting a car off her infant. Physical reactions are accompanied by feelings of threat. Usually the person or animal copes or the stressor is removed, and the alarm reaction subsides.

If the shock is intense and/or prolonged, the individual enters the resistance stage. The body seems to recover from the alarm, adrenaline secretion declines, and secretion of the pituitary hormone ACTH increases, as do the hormones from the adrenal cortex, noradrenaline (norepinephrine), and cortisone. Again, if the pressures continue, and if coping mechanisms are insufficient, the person enters the exhaustion stage, in which the adrenal glands no longer function and physical symptoms, such as collapse, or psychological symptoms, such as depression and withdrawal, appear. At the extreme, the person may die.

Case 1:3. Bill Stone was a patrolman in a large eastern city. An alcoholic, he got off the midnight shift, changed into civilian clothes, and made the round of his favorite bars. Finally, a bartender refused to serve him. He emptied the rounds from his weapon and handed them to the bartender. Then he wove his way down the street to a uniform store.

In the uniform store, he took out his weapon and waved it around. (His back was to the door and the plate glass window that faced the street). While the employees knew him and were not badly frightened, they still were apprehensive and were trying to persuade him to "put the gun down, Billy, and have a cup of coffee."

As luck would have it, another officer, Charles Rocco, also in plain clothes, was coming down the street on his way to the store. He was from another precinct and did not know Stone. A citizen looking through the window saw a man waving a gun. He began running and yelling that there was a robbery in progress. Rocco raced to the store, saw the same scene, and yelled, "Police! Drop the gun!" Stone, vaguely hearing a noise outside, wheeled around, weapon still in hand, so that it now was pointing directly at Rocco. Rocco fired, striking Stone in the arm. He rushed in to administer first aid and found Stone's badge and identification papers.

The next day Rocco collapsed and was admitted to the hospital with irregular heartbeat, pains in his chest, and breathing trouble. These were found to be symptoms of an acute anxiety attack. He was hospitalized for several days.

Recent criticisms of Selye's work have attacked his idea that the physical response to stressors is nonspecific and particularly have shown the importance of psychological factors, including attitudes and beliefs. They have shown that the stages are not unvarying and may be short-circuited by an intense or overwhelming stressor, or they may be foreshortened or prolonged depending on the intensity and/or duration of the stressor and the state of the organism at the time of exposure (Cofer and Appley, 1964; Monat and Lazarus, 1977).

The specific physiological events by which stress-related physical diseases develop is still uncertain. This is the province of psychosomatic medicine, and a detailed discussion of current theories in that field is beyond the scope of this book. It is probable, however, that psychosomatic disease is in some way related to the physiological changes of the GAS, particularly in those cases in which coping is only partly successful so that the body has chronically high levels of adrenaline, noradrenaline, and the glucocorticoid hormones (including hydrocortisone, corticosterone, and cortisone). The latter group seems to be particularly important in that it interferes with the body's ability to form disease-fighting antibodies and decreases the number of white blood cells, which also help to fight infection. The sex hormones also decrease, accounting in part, perhaps, for the often-reported decline in sexual interest when one is depressed or under pressure (Coleman, Butcher, and Carson, 1980).

Physicians are becoming more aware that the presence of disease organisms alone are not enough to bring on symptoms. As biologist-philosopher René Dubos (1965) puts it, "The microbial diseases most common today arise from the activity of microorganisms that are ubiquitous in the environment . . . and exert pathological effects only when the infected person is under conditions of physiological stress." For example, many people in the United States harbor the tuberculosis bacillus, but few show symptoms of this once-dreaded killer.

In addition to the possibility of a direct connection between the physiological reactions to stress and illness, several less direct links are possible (Monat and Lazarus, 1977). The person who is under pressure may engage

> in coping activities that are damaging to health, for example, by trying to advance occupationally or socially by means of a pressured style of life, by taking minimal rest, by poor diet, heavy use of tobacco or alcohol, etc. Intrinsically noxious styles of living can increase the likelihood of disease by damaging the tissues of the body. A third way stress might lead to disease is by psychological and/or sociological factors which consistently lead the person to minimize the significance of various symptoms. That is, a person may frequently interpret pain or illness symptoms in such a way as to neglect to seek medical aid when it is crucial. Avoidance of doctors or of medical regimens can come about as a defense mechanism, for example, denial, or merely because the individual is a member of a culture or subculture that values stoicism. Such avoidance can be fatal in certain instances, such as in the case of heart attack victims who delay seeking medical attention, thereby decreasing their chances of survival (p. 5) /references deleted/.

Not only can stress increase susceptibility to disease, but disease, especially chronic disease, can itself be a stressor. A host of diseases have been connected to stress; indeed, it has been estimated that 80 percent of all people who come to physicians complain of disorders that are to some degree psychosomatic (Coleman, Butcher, and Carson, 1980). Many of the health problems believed to be connected to stress are mild and transitory, colds being one example. Still, the evidence of a relationship between stress and disease is suggestive enough to cause concern and lead to a search for palliative measures by industry and individuals. Following is a list of some of the disorders believed to be related to stress.

Stress-related Disorders

Cardiovascular disorders
    hypertension (high blood pressure)
    tachycardia
    acute myocardial infarction (heart attack)
Skin problems
    rashes
    hives
    pruritis (itching)
    herpes
Disorders of the musculoskeletal system
    backache (low-back syndrome)
    muscle cramps
    tension headaches (including migraines)
    stiff neck
Respiratory disease
    bronchial asthma
    hyperventilation syndrome
    tuberculosis
Gastrointestinal disorders
    peptic ulcer
    chronic gastritis
    ulcerative and mucous colitis
    constipation
    hyperacidity
    pyloric spasm
    "heartburn"
    irritable colon
    spastic esophagus

Genitourinary disorders
  disturbances in urination
  disturbances in sexual functioning
Endocrine disorders
  diabetes mellitus
  thyroid disorders
  adrenal disorders
  pituitary disorders
  menstrual disorders
Others
  cancer

Psychological Responses to Stressful Events

In addition to the physiological reactions, stress has a psychological component. As discussed earlier, when a person is under pressure, when a person feels threatened, he searches for ways to deal with that threat. These may be either task oriented or defensive. Often they succeed, and the person returns to normal. Sometimes, however, changes come too quickly or the threat is too severe, and the person is pushed beyond his limits so that ordinary ways of acting, reacting, and thinking are inadequate. This situation has been called a crisis.

Like the term stress, crisis has been used several ways. According to one definition, crisis is "a limited period in which an individual . . . is exposed to threats or demands which are at or near the limits of his resources" (Lazarus, 1966, p. 407). A slightly different definition calls it "a subjective reaction to a stressful life experience, one so affecting the stability of the individual that the ability to cope or function may be seriously compromised" (Bard and Ellison, 1974, p. 68). Both of these definitions have in common the theme of disruption and chaos.

Another common feature of crisis is that it is believed to be a time when people are especially susceptible to change, which can prove to be a turning point in their lives, one from which they may emerge with psychological damage or with greater strength and ability to cope with future stressful events (Bard and Ellison, 1974).

Crisis can come from all the kinds of stressors, as described previously: the normal developmental stressors, such as marriage or retirement, the accidental stressors of sudden illness, crime victimization, or natural disaster, or the chronic stressors of disruptive, chaotic family, neighborhood, or job. With the developmental stressors and the chronic stressors, pressure may build slowly, with chronic feelings of low-level anxiety and malaise. This state may be punctuated from time to time by periods of acute distress — of crisis. These acute crisis periods can be triggered by any number of events, "straws that break the camel's back," which may not be related to what is really bothering the person and may be something he ordinarily handles well. It is at times such as this that symptoms of psychological distress flare up, sometimes expressed in depression, sudden outbursts of temper, alcoholic binges, crying jags, domestic disputes, and even suicide attempts or psychotic episodes.[9]

Reactions in Crisis

People's overt reactions in crisis vary tremendously; thus, no one kind of behavior is evidence that a person is or is not in a crisis state. A list of reactions commonly seen in crises follows.

Behavior in Crisis

anger	depression
anxiety attacks	desire for action
apathy	desire for revenge
changes in sexual response	disbelief
compulsive actions	disrupted eating habits
confusion	disrupted sleeping patterns
crying jags	distrust
denial	extreme calm
dependence, clinging	fear
feelings of going crazy	obsessive thoughts
frustration	panic
guilt	phobias
headaches	repression
hypersensitivity	self-hatred
laughing, joking	shock
nightmares	skin reactions: hives and so forth

There is a particular problem if the person seems to be extremely calm or even is laughing and joking in a situation where the appropriate reaction would be grief, hysteria, or the like. Others tend to believe such a person is not upset; in these situations they may not give needed support and may even condemn him for acting "inappropriately" (Silver and Wortman, 1980). This is sometimes seen at funerals, where a family member may tell little jokes, or with victims of sexual assault, who describe the situation in what appear to be matter-of-fact terms. "It's a disgrace!" say scandalized neighbors. "Al must not have loved his mother." "Alice must be lying," the emergency room staff says. "No one who was really raped would be that calm."

Another reaction that is sometimes seen and needs explanation is the tendency to identify with the aggressor. This behavior was originally described in concentration camp inmates; today it is particularly prevalent in cases in which there have been long periods of interaction between a victim and offender, such as kidnapping or hostage taking. The victim, owing his life and physical safety to the caprice of the offender, is relieved and grateful to be alive. Many react with extreme passivity and even come to feel sorry for the offender or to express positive feelings toward him. In hostage taking this is called the "Stockholm syndrome," after a situation in Sweden in which a hostage fell in love with a man who had held her and others for several days under unpleasant conditions.

Despite the variety of reactions, there seem to be several constant elements. Just as there are stages in physiological reactions, so crisis reactions often occur in stages. These stages are extremely variable, however; the stage that lasts a few days for one person may last weeks for another.

The first stage, the acute crisis phase, begins with the precipitating incident and typically, at least with accidental stressors, lasts a few hours, or perhaps a day. Reactions include denial ("There must be some mistake." "This isn't happening to me.") and disruption. The person feels anxious, threatened, and out of control. His life seems to be in chaos.

Another common reaction in the acute crisis phase is guilt. The guilt may be straightforward, "I must have done something wrong," or it may be projected onto another person. An example of the latter phenomenon is seen in the burglary victim who, feeling guilty because he left the house unlocked, tells the responding officer angrily,

"If you had been out there doing your job instead of giving out tickets, this wouldn't have happened to me."

The person in crisis also may regress and act and think in more childlike ways. As a result, he cannot be expected to think and act rationally. This is why people who work in jobs that involve dealing with life-and-death situations are carefully trained so that they will react instinctively and not be thrown into crisis. Sometimes even this training is insufficient.

> **Case 1:4.** A patrolman with six years' experience responded to a situation in which a man had committed suicide by jumping off an overpass onto a busy highway. He had been hit by several cars, and his body cut to pieces. The largest piece included his head, part of his chest, and one arm. The patrolman ran to this piece, picked up the arm, and tried to find a pulse.

In crisis, perceptions are distorted. People do not forget that a certain incident took place, but the details may be fuzzy. Alternatively, details that seem burned into someone's memory may be completely inaccurate. Research in eyewitness testimony shows that the information given by people under stress is particularly likely to be unreliable (Ellison and Buckout, 1981). Thus, time perception usually is inaccurate, ten minutes seem like twenty, and an hour like two.

A woman who teaches crisis management to police officers tells the following personal story to illustrate the irrationality and distorted perception of crisis.

> **Case 1:5.** I think of myself as a very rational person, and I have a healthy respect for firearms. I grew up in a small southern town where Sunday afternoon's recreation was sitting on the riverbank shooting rats. I was given a .22 rifle when I was ten and was a fair shot. I have also worked in emergency rooms and seen the damage bullets can do to humans. Before this incident, if anyone had asked me what I would do were I to be confronted by a gunman, I would have said, "I'd give him anything he wants, no argument, and just hope that he goes

away."

My husband and I were moving and were taking the last load to the van when an armed man appeared and demanded our money. I had none. I looked around me, then took the object I was holding — it was a catsup bottle — and threw it at him. It hit him, the top came off, the catsup spewed all over the place, and the bottle hit the ground and broke with a loud bang. Believing I was shot, I fell down and began to scream.

The police came — it seemed to take forever for them to get there — and began to question us. They started with my husband, and I listened astonished as he told of taking his wallet out and throwing it on the ground just before I let fly. I did not see or remember any of that. I did remember the weapon, but it couldn't have been that little thing they found on the suspect using our credit cards. It must have been at least a sawed-off shotgun.

A poignant example of the disruption and distorted perceptions of crisis comes in Wambaugh's (1973) account of the murder of an officer, *The Onion Field*. Again and again he speaks of the missing piece of evidence: No one remembered who had the gun.

The person in crisis is open, vulnerable, and suggestible. His "defenses are down." This is why the reactions of others, and the interpretations they put on the events, are particularly powerful, and change can be rapid and striking.

The needs of people in the acute crisis phase often are relatively straightforward. They are, not surprisingly, the same conditions that minimize the stressful impact of events in the first place and those that lessen one's chance of being thrown into crisis. First, because part of the disruption of crisis is the perception of loss of control, there is the need to have some feeling of regaining control over one's life. This usually involves a belief that one can do something to make the situation better. When the disruption has been severe, as from the loss of a child or spouse, the feeling of control regained may come slowly. At first it may help if others take over some of the decision making.[10]

The effects of the need to regain control are sometimes seen in the behavior of crime victims. If an interviewer is aggressive in his attempt to get information, the victim may view him in much the same way he did the offender, thinking that he is trying to force something from him. In these cases it is not uncommon for victims to become actively uncooperative, to be unable to remember details, or to supply inaccurate details in the hope of satisfying the investigator and getting the officer to leave him alone. By the same token, the officer who shows concern for the victim's welfare by phrases such as, "Are you all right? Do you think you can talk to us now?" and who in this way gives the victim some perception of control over the interview is much more likely to get cooperation and accurate information. He also lessens the chances that the victim will suffer long-term trauma from the event.[11]

Again, support from one's social network helps put perspective on the event and provides options for dealing with it. Most of the literature written for people involved in crisis intervention, especially those who work on telephone "hot lines," seems to stress passivity and the importance of not giving suggestions and directions. Although this may be appropriate in long-term therapy, the authors have found that, especially in the first hours after a traumatic event, a much more active, directive approach works better. Many of the people with whom the authors work are too confused and paralyzed to know what they are thinking and feeling or what they need. More than anything else they want someone to help them understand the situation and to give them information about their options. The ability to be both active and at the same time to allow the victim a feeling of control is one of the more delicate, difficult tasks facing the crisis worker. Keys to this ability include giving the victim a sense of control over how something is to happen, if not over what is to happen, and presenting information and options without making the decisions.

A topic that has been much discussed in writings about crisis is ventilation. Some people in crisis find they cope and recover better if they have the opportunity to ventilate. Ventilation means to "get it out of one's system." For adults this is usually done by talking about what has happened and about one's feelings: the fears, the anger, the guilt, and so forth.

Some crisis theorists seem to believe that any pouring forth of feelings is sufficient and that the proper stance of the listener should be one of nonjudgmental passivity. As was previously discussed, the authors do not agree with this view. Ventilation that focuses constantly on the person's misery, that dwells obsessively on the crisis-producing event, with emphasis on all the things one should have done differently, can, we believe, do more harm than good. As part of the process of talking about what has happened, one also needs to make some plans for the future, plans that involve creative ways to cope with present stressors and minimize the impact of future ones. This is how crisis can lead to growth.

Finally, some people seem to prefer to work things out on their own, without discussing it with others. Certainly attempts to force such a person to discuss his feelings or to hint directly that dreadful consequences await those who bottle up their thoughts and feelings are inappropriate. There is no evidence that suppressing thoughts of unpleasant events inevitably leads to subsequent problems. Again, the choice should be the client's.

Crisis is also made easier if the person understands what is happening and why and is able to know what to expect. One of the things many people in crisis can expect is that it will take some time to recover. Indeed, after a particularly severe stressor, such as loss of a spouse or parent, one is never the same again. People know this and are comforted if someone else assures them that their perceptions are accurate.

A second phase commonly seen in people who have been in crisis involves attempts at integrating the traumatic event into their lives and self-concepts. At first this may be a phase of false recovery. The person feels that everything is all right, that he is coping and has recovered. He wants to get on with living, to try to forget what has happened, and does not want to talk about it. We call this the denial/integration stage.

Commonly, however, this feeling is interrupted by a third phase, one characterized by flashbacks, more formally called "secondary crisis reactions" (Sutherland and Scherl, 1970). The person remembers the crisis-producing event and relives the emotional experiences. Nightmares, irrational fears, shakiness, and changes in eating and sleeping habits, common in the first day or so after the event, may return. Depression and hypersensitivity may begin and the person fears that he is going crazy and will never recover. One common flashback symptom found among police is a sort of hallucination in which the officer can smell again scents associated with a grisly scene, particularly the scents of a decaying body (known in the jargon as "ripe DOA").

When flashbacks occur, the officer may want to talk to someone about it. At the very least, he usually is helped if he has been warned during the acute crisis phase that this might happen and is reassured that it is a natural phase in what is essentially a mourning process, not evidence that he is going crazy, is weak, or cannot cope.[12]

Flashbacks may come at predictable times for obvious reasons. People who have lost a spouse, for example, usually have flashbacks around the dates that were important to the relationship: birthdays, anniversaries, major holidays such as Thanksgiving, and the like. Crime victims often have them when confronted with lineups or the need to testify. The senior author has known several victims of sexual assault who experienced flashbacks when they passed the spot where they were assaulted or even when they heard a lecture or saw a television program about rape.

Flashbacks also may seem to occur for no discernible reason. This kind, because of its unpredictability, is particularly distressing.

The last two phases of reaction to crisis, denial/integration and flashback, may alternate for some time. The denial/integration phases vary enormously in duration. The authors have seen people go for months or even years without a major flashback, only to be hit with one of extreme intensity. It is the authors' general experience that people who have several flashbacks rather close to each other soon after the traumatic event are somewhat less likely to have major flashbacks in later months. Under favorable circumstances, if the person's needs are met, the flashbacks become less frequent and less severe, until he feels totally recovered. This process can take a few hours or days with mild stressors and appropriate personal resources and social support and several years with more severe stressors, such as the loss of a family member.

During flashbacks, the person in crisis again may need the help and support of those with whom he interacts and whom he trusts. With such help, he can become stronger and better able to cope. Without it, and without personal strengths, the normal defense mechanisms, which arose to help him cope, become permanent features of his behavior that can hinder his long-range ability to deal with future stressors. The nightmares one expects after being involved either as a helper or a victim in a particularly grisly wreck do not lessen in intensity but become a permanent part of one's sleep.

Crisis, then, provides particularly dramatic evidence of the impact of events on people's psychological functioning. It has become a cliché that crisis involves both danger and opportunity (Bard, 1974), and the nature of intervention in crisis can have long-range effects on abilities to cope with stressors.

Summary

Stress is an inevitable part of life. Stressors come in many forms, some within the individual, others in the environment. Indeed, according to the classic theory, any change is stressful to some extent.

Not all change, however, necessarily leads to harmful consequences. With certain exceptions, which are rare in our society, it is possible for most people to cope successfully with pressures. Successful coping by individuals is made easier if the environment in which they live and work offers them support and succor. A feedback loop comes into play, so success leads to future success and failure to future harm.

To be most successful, then, stress management must involve analysis — and possibly change — at a number of levels, organizational as well as individual. Later in this book the authors will describe some of the solutions that are consistent with theory and are reported by researchers and practitioners to have met with some measure of success. Again, there is still much controversy in the field and much to be done. Certainly there is no 100 percent formula for success and happiness. (Indeed, happiness is probably a process, not an end point or object. Most of us find that once we achieve one goal that we thought would bring happiness we begin to work on others.) The lack of a guarantee is, however, no excuse for avoiding action.

The space devoted to this discussion of the nature of stress comes from the authors' belief that understanding is a first step in the control that is a crucial part of stress management. This is the base for consistent action.

NOTES

1. In Heron's study, in which students were subjected to sensory deprivation in a laboratory, half the subjects asked to be released within forty-eight hours.

2. It is unclear whether this is a global, unchanging personality trait or whether it changes with time and circumstance.

3. Rotter tends to believe that locus of control is a global, enduring personality trait that characterizes the individual's general outlook. Others argue that locus of control may be situational.

4. This discussion is drawn largely from Gergen and Gergen (1981).

5. For a more complete discussion of the complexities of predictability as a stress reducer, see Matthews et al. (1979).

6. In most of the case histories in this book, names and locations will be changed. The exception will be those cases in which a specific, actual town or department is mentioned, e.g. Lt. John Genz of the New Jersey State Police.

7. This and similar case histories, while interesting, must be taken largely for their power as illustrative anecdotes. The authors realize that they are correlational and that other factors, such as prior problems and the person's definition of the situation, must be taken into account.

8. Here, again, with correlational data one cannot assume a cause-effect relationship. It may be that heavy smoking and the other factors are characteristics of people who choose jobs working with other people.

9. The authors present here the model they have found useful in working with people in crisis, especially crisis caused by accidental stressors. For an excellent analysis of other models, see Silver and Wortman (1980).

10. In these circumstances, the authors have always found it appropriate, when in doubt, to ask what our "client" wants. The authors are also relentless about encouraging the person to make his own decisions as soon as possible so as neither to seem to be rescuers nor to teach the person in crisis to be inappropriately, chronically dependent.

11. For a more complete discussion of this process, see Ellison

and Buckhout (1981).

12. The authors sometimes use the analogy of a surgical incision or accidental cut that hurts at first, then stops hurting for a while, then itches or aches so painfully that the initial pain seems mild by comparison.

Chapter 2

STRESS IN POLICING

Introduction

A GROWING body of literature emphasizes the emotional hazards of police work. A government-sponsored bibliography on police stress (Duncan, Brenner, and Kravitz, 1979) lists 133 articles and 33 training films on the subject. A journal has been devoted to it. Somodevilla and his colleagues (1978) have called policing "the most emotionally hazardous job of all," and Hans Selye himself (1978) said that "police work . . . ranks as one of the most hazardous professions, even exceeding the formidable stresses and strains of air traffic control."

While much has been claimed, little has been demonstrated conclusively. The first problem comes in deciding how to measure the relative stressfulness of different jobs. One measure frequently used is self-report of stress. In these studies, workers are asked to rate the job's stressfulness and to describe the parts of their jobs that they find most bothersome.

Kroes, Margolis, and Hurrell (1974) reported the responses of 100 Cincinnati police officers to questions of stress in their jobs. They listed problems with administration of the department as the most bothersome pressures. High on the list of administrative hassles were offensive policies, lack of participation in decision making, and difficult work schedules. In a subsequent study of California officers who had come to a clinic for psychological help, Kroes and Gould (1981) found somewhat different items mentioned. Particularly important with this group was lack of support from the administration, an area of little importance to the Cincinnati officers. The Californians went so far as to describe active efforts on the part of administrators to "get" an individual. These officers also found difficulty dealing with tragedies on the street and with job-related injuries.

Sewell (1981) attacked the question somewhat differently. He constructed a questionnaire of 144 events commonly experienced by officers and had students at the FBI National Academy and members of a Virginia county police department rate their stressfulness on a scale of 1 to 100, using changing work shifts, with an arbitrary value of 50, as an anchor.[1] Items rated most stressful were violent death of a partner in the line of duty, with a mean score of 88, dismissal (85), taking a life in the line of duty (84), shooting someone in the line of duty (81), and suicide of an officer who is a close friend (80). No attempt was made to determine whether any of the officers participating had actually experienced any of these events and whether such experience influenced the results, nor despite the author's stated attempts to construct a comparable scale can the items on this scale be added to those of the Holmes and Rahe Stressful Life Events (SLE) Scale to give a comprehensive score. The use of different anchors makes comparison inappropriate; indeed, on the one item the two scales have in common, "vacation," the SLE rating is 13, and that on Sewell's measure is 20.

Two hundred twenty-three male officers from three Texas departments, studied by Price and his colleagues (1978), listed the following items as the most tense duties they performed:

1. Officer needs assistance
2. Robbery in progress
3. High speed auto chase
4. Person with gun
5. Mentally disturbed person
6. Shooting
7. Child beating
8. Family fights/disturbances
9. Possible homicide

10. Unknown nature of call

Pendergrass and Ostrove (1982) used the Spielberger Police Stress Survey to compare male and female officers from Maryland departments on ratings of stressful events. (The standard used here was "Assignment of disagreeable duty" = 50.) Male officers listed the following as most stressful:

1. Fellow officer killed in the line of duty (82.2)
2. Killing someone in the line of duty (75.4)
3. Exposure to dead or battered children (73.4)
4. Inadequate support by department (70.4)
5. Insufficient manpower to handle a job adequately (69.9)
6. Competition for or lack of advancement (67.9)
7. Physical attack on one's person (66.6)
8. Changing shift hours (64.5)

Female officers gave a somewhat different list:

1. Killing someone in the line of duty (94.1)
2. Fellow officer killed in line of duty (88.2)
3. Exposure to battered or dead children (82.2)
4. Insufficient manpower to handle a job adequately (79.5)
5. Physical attacks on one's person (79.4)
6. Inadequate support by department (75.1)
7. Making arrests while alone (73.5)
8. Responding to a felony in progress (73.4)

Most of this research studied only police officers and did not compare them with workers in other occupations. One study that did make such comparisons found that responsibility for others, complexity of work, low salaries, and lack of participation in decision making were thought to be particularly stressful to police (French, 1975). However, French's work seemed to indicate that the pressures of police work were neither extreme nor particularly worse than those of other occupations.

Silbert's (1982) work partially confirms French's. She compared San Francisco officers with one to five years of service with a group of human service professionals and a mixed group of other professionals. She found that the officers reported being more highly stressed by their jobs and believed that they were underpaid and that their work was not recognized or appreciated properly. They were generally less satisfied with their work than the other groups but had fewer of the symptoms of burnout. Lack of support, administrative hassles such as paperwork and red tape, the physical danger of the job, combined with inadequate tangible rewards and appreciation for their performance, were among their major stressors. The authors question whether the groups in this study are the best comparison groups for police. They are generally from different socioeconomic backgrounds, are better educated, and are given more autonomy in their jobs. It is also possible that some of these findings are due to demand characteristics: that police, more than other groups, are expected to gripe. Certainly, compared to other occupations whose members have similar educational and socioeconomic backgrounds, the pay of police objectively is not particularly bad.

Comparing police officers with civilian dispatchers in the same department, Pendergrass and Ostrove (1982) found higher levels of both physiological and psychological complaints among the dispatchers than among officers. This was true for both male and female employees. Officers reported psychological problems such as cynicism, low self-esteem, and sleepiness on the job an average of 12.03 weeks a year, while dispatchers reported them in 15.8 weeks. Health problems, such as chest pains, headaches, muscle tension, and nausea were reported a mean of 12.85 weeks by sworn officers and 20.35 weeks by dispatchers.

There is even evidence of strong positive aspects to the job of policing. The officers that French questioned felt secure in their jobs and believed that they had opportunities to use their talents. They were higher on job satisfaction than most of the other groups studied and were less likely to be bored. Other work finds that police officers are generally emotionally stable and have a temperament that is below average in neuroticism and anxiety (Reiser, 1973; Blackmore, 1978). Officers generally consider themselves to be in good health (Terry, 1981). As Terry observes, "If police work is as highly stressful as it is portrayed to be, one would not expect to find these sentiments and personal attributes" (p. 63).

Another sort of measure of the pressures of a job counts the incidence of diseases and disorders that are believed to be stress related. In particular, claims abound of excessive rates of suicide, divorce, and cardiovascular, respiratory, and gastrointestinal diseases among officers, but more than thirty-five physiological states and any number of psychological problems have been attributed to job-related stressors (Terry, 1981). One study of 2,300 officers in twenty-nine departments found that 36 percent had serious health problems (Blackmore, 1978).

Other, less serious, health problems also have been reported frequently among police. Silbert's (1982) sample complained of having headaches, being fidgety or tense, having backaches, being "nervous or shaky inside," having stomach aches, losing appetite on duty, having problems with falling or staying asleep, and having nightmares. Price and his collegues (1978) found that back problems were a major reason for early retirement.

Other studies have compared health problems of police officers with those of people in other occupations. Lester (1981) found that the rates for injuries and illnesses reported by Connecticut police officers (43.7 per 100 workers in 1978) were higher than for any other occupation (the overall rate was 9.7). The rate for California officers in 1977 was 23.9, compared with 22.9 for fire protection workers, 34.2 for sanitary services, and 10.0 for all employees.[2] Richard and Fell (1975) also found that Tennessee police were admitted to hospitals at a higher rate than other workers but that they were not more likely than other groups to seek help at mental health facilities. Blackmore (1978) concurs that admissions of police to hospitals are high, ranking thirteen out of 130 occupations studied.

While Terry (1981) admits that police have high rates for several illnesses, he concludes that "law enforcement no longer stands above all other occupations in terms of physiological maladies" (p. 66). He further suggests that social class may be more important than specific occupation in determining physiological illnesses.

In addition to physiological consequences, pressure is believed to lead to problems in psychological adaptation. Problems in living that have been attributed to the stressful nature of policing include suicide, marital and family problems, sex problems from impotence to promiscuity, unnecessary risk taking, isolation from friends, particularly friends who are not police, callousness, alcoholism, extortion and other criminal behavior, and unnecessary violence in dealing with citizens. Here, too, data are scarce, and the methodology of those studies which have appeared often is seriously flawed. The areas of this poor lot that have been studied most fully are suicide, divorce, and alcoholism.

Several studies seem to show that, compared to workers in other occupations, police officers are particularly prone to kill themselves. Indeed, officers are much more likely to die by their own hands than to be killed by others (Kroes, 1976).[3] Using data gathered during periods ranging from the 1930s through the 1960s, several authors have found high rates of police suicide, among them Heiman (1975), who studied officers in Chicago, San Francisco, and New York; Niederhoffer (1967), who studied New York officers; Nelson and Smith (1970) for Wyoming; Richard and Fell (1975) for Tennessee; and Guralnick (1963) and Labovitz and Hagedorn (1971), who used United States census data.

These studies vary, however, in whether policing was found to have the highest suicide rate among the occupations studied. In studies that used data from 1950, Guralnick (1963) found police to have the highest rates, while Kroes (1976) found police committed suicide less frequently than laborers and lumbermen but somewhat more frequently than physicians, and Labovitz and Hagedorn (1971) reported them as being surpassed only by self-employed manufacturing managers. Richard and Fell (1975) found police third behind laborers and pressmen.[4]

Rates also seem to vary tremendously from department to department. Despite Wambaugh's frequent inclusion of police suicides in his novels about the Los Angeles police department, on examining figures from that department, Dash and Reiser (1978) argued that they were not particularly high. Denver and London also are reported to have low rates (Terry, 1981). Heiman (1977) states that, in general, police suicides are less common in the Midwest and South than in the East and West.

While the consensus seems to be that, overall, officers are higher than average in the tendency to commit suicide, this area has been a particularly difficult one in which to gather evidence. Departments either do not keep accurate data or are reluctant to release it (Heiman, 1977). Some (Kroes, 1976) believe that the police suicide rate is artificially low due to a tendency of departments to report any death that can possibly be viewed in another way as accidental. It is equally possible to argue that police suicides are particularly likely to be reported because of their overwhelming preference for using guns; certainly this method is much less easy to rationalize than overdoses of drugs.

Specific information about the nature of suicides by police officers is especially difficult to obtain. The two studies that do report
such evidence (Friedman [1968], who studied the New York police
department's statistics in the late 1930s and Danto [1978], using De-
troit data from 1968 to 1976) concur that alcohol abuse is common
and that marital trouble is the most important precipitating stressor.
As always with correlational data, extreme caution must be used in
asserting that marital trouble causes suicide. Family problems and
suicide may both be linked to a common bond, such as depression.

As noted, firearms are the most common method of suicide in
police officers. This is consistent with a "macho" image and may
mean that police suicides are more likely to be successful than those
of other groups, who are more prone to use less intrinsically lethal
means such as drugs, carbon monoxide, and wrist slashing.

Information about alcohol abuse among police is even more difficult to obtain than are suicide statistics, but it is generally believed to
be high. In his study of 2,300 officers, Blackmore (1978) found that
23 percent had serious alcohol problems, while Bennett-Sandler and
Ubell (1977) claim that over 1,000 officers from the New York City
police department sought help for alcoholism (under orders) in 1976
(out of a department of more than 25,000), and Kroes (1976) states
that "in one major police department over 20% of the officers had a
serious drinking problem" (p. 82).[5] Over half of the officers questioned by Price and his colleagues (1978) reported that alcohol had
caused problems among their closest friends. There is no evidence in
this literature on how this compares with other occupations.

A leading text on police supervision warns that "by its very nature, police work is conducive to problem drinking" (Iannone,
1980). Not only is pressure common in the job, but drinking also is
very much a part of the police subculture. Many officers regularly
end their tours of duty at a bar, often one frequented primarily by
police. Alcohol provides an approved way to unwind and acts as a
lubricant for conversation. Unfortunately, because officers usually
are armed, drunken brawls at parties and taverns pose a special risk.
The anecdotal evidence commonly known as "war stories" is full of
incidents of dangerous behavior by drunken officers. In one recent
incident in New Jersey, two officers were "horsing around" with
loaded, cocked weapons at a party. Both had been drinking heavily
most of the day. In the course of this horseplay, one was shot and

killed.

Several studies (Hillgren, Bond, and Jones, 1976; Kroes, Margolis, and Hurrell, 1974; Blackmore, 1978) report that officers find the job disruptive to their family lives. Again, no evidence is given of how this compares with people in other occupations.

Divorce, of course, is perhaps the clearest evidence of family problems, and studies about its extent among police contradict each other, or at least show large differences among departments. Durner, Kroeker, Miller, and Reynolds (1975) found police divorce rates to be 17 percent in Baltimore, 27 percent in Santa Ana, California, and 33.3 percent in Chicago. Baxter (1978) finds similar numbers, with a national rate of 30 percent. Based on data from the 1970 census, Blackmore (1978) reports that 22 percent of the police officers sampled had been divorced at least once, a figure much higher than the average of 13.8 percent for all groups. Officers who were married before they came on the job were much more likely to be divorced (26%) than those who married after entering police work (11%).

In contrast to these data, Reiser found low divorce rates among LAPD officers, and Kroes, Margolis, and Hurrell (1974) state that only 5 percent of the officers they interviewed were divorced. Data gathered prior to 1970 are particularly likely to show low rates (Whitehouse, 1965; Bayley and Mendelsohn, 1969; Watson and Sterling, 1969).

It seems, then, that although divorce among police may be higher than the national average, it is not as rampant as some writers would have us believe. Even at this it is difficult to use these data unequivocally as evidence of the effects of the pressures of the job because few studies asked whether the officer was married or divorced before he came on the job, and none give information about multiple divorces.

Thus, the data seem to show that, while there are many stressful situations in policing, and although, as Terry (1981) says, "Problems are found in large enough numbers to be of concern," there is little evidence to support the extravagant claims that policing is the most stressful of modern occupations. Hope also comes from the evidence that there is enormous variation among departments in the incidence of ailments believed to be caused by stress.

In a more specific discussion of factors thought to contribute to stress in police, several authors (Stratton, 1978; Ellison and Genz, 1978; Blackmore, 1978; Wallace, 1978; Grencik, 1975) resort to four general categories: (1) stressors external to the police organization, (2) stressors inherent in the police role, (3) stressors in the organizational structure and in supervisory style, and (4) stressors resulting from individual personalities.[6] Within these categories, many situations are listed. The authors will describe some of these in the pages that follow and include anecdotal evidence from their own experience. However, it is important to remember that there is very little evidence of the relative frequency or importance of each of these, so these lists must be seen as suggestive rather than definitive.

Stressors External to the Police Organization

Police work is carried on in the wider contexts of both the criminal justice system and a community. Events and situations in these contexts often influence the way an officer must do his job and even the way that job is defined.

STRESSORS IN THE CRIMINAL JUSTICE SYSTEM. One of the most commonly heard complaints from police officers concerns the larger legal system in which they work (Kroes, 1976; Stratton, 1978). There is a common perception that police are beleaguered, are caught between a hostile public and hosts of criminals on one side and laws, courts, and correctional systems that are inefficient at best, and at worst hostile, i.e. siding with the public and the perpetrator, on the other.

It is indeed accurate that the Constitution puts the burden of proof on the state and that the accused is presumed innocent until proven guilty. Supreme Court decisions of the 1960s strengthened this presumption. However, despite police expectations, these decisions did not lead to empty prisons, although their actual impact on convictions has never been assessed. Police often perceive this constitutional restraint as being in conflict with their mandate to protect society and help bring the guilty to justice (Broderick, 1977). As George Kirkham (1974), a criminology professor who became a police officer and whose perceptions of policing changed radically in the process, puts it,

> The toughest adversary a street cop must confront each day is not the armed robber or enraged mob, not the addict, the burglar or mugger.

Rather it is, ironically, the very law which he must struggle against increasingly difficult odds to enforce. It is the smugness and complacency of courts and legislatures which spin out a hopelessly entangling web of procedural restraints upon men who are charged with the awesome responsibility of protecting our society.

Changes in the law, or in interpretations of the law, at times happen quickly. A department with a large legal staff may be able to keep abreast of these changes and keep officers informed, but the average department lacks these facilities, so the officer may be unaware of a change or nuance in the law until he is confronted with it in court.

Tactics of defense attorneys also arouse ire. Although numerous continuances of a case may result in increased overtime pay for the officer involved, this officer, who has been preparing himself for the court confrontation, may find himself standing idly outside the courtroom and then dismissed. Once on the stand, the defense attorney will attempt to discredit his testimony and even to make him appear foolish or guilty of some malfeasance himself. Defense tactics that lead to acquittal or dismissal on a technicality also are irksome to many, especially when the officer is fairly certain that the suspect is guilty and regards the crime as heinous.

Police perceive special leniency toward suspects in other areas. The bail system allows some suspects to be free before the officer has finished his paperwork. He may see a case on which he has worked hard plea bargained at what he considers an outrageous level and may not even be informed of this disposition. (Officers often forget, in these situations, that part of the game is to pile on a plethora of charges in the expectation of losing some in the process.) Many officers also feel that juries and judges are susceptible to the stories of defendants, who have been cleaned up and made presentable by their attorneys, and that when a conviction is obtained, sentences do not fit the crime. (It is interesting to note here that defense attorneys have the opposite perception of the same events: they feel that the odds favor the police, who will create or destroy evidence or otherwise falsify testimony in order to close a case, to put away an individual whom they dislike.)[7]

The authors believe that some of these attitudes may be traced to problems in training. In some states the required training period for police officers is only six weeks. Even when it is doubled or quadrupled (which is more common), little time is devoted to more than rote understanding of the provisions of the Bill of Rights (or the historical circumstances that led to such guarantees). Few academies have the luxury of instructors who are both competent constitutional lawyers and good teachers.

Many officers are encouraged in a simplistic belief of themselves as knights in shining armor. They are encouraged to expect respect and obedience and to see themselves as the law rather than as agents in its enforcement. In the authors' experience, the realities of the court system are not often impressed on recruits, so they arrive on the streets with misconceptions of what their job is and of what is actually possible.

STRESSORS IN THE COMMUNITY. In addition to pressures from the criminal justice system, police often are sensitive to pressures from the community. Stressors of this sort may come from several sources, one being the political atmosphere. Politicians not infrequently put pressure both on individual officers and on the department as a whole to ignore, bend, or change policy or to grant special privileges and favors. Politicians also have been known to use real or exaggerated problems in the police department to further their own careers.

A different kind of pressure comes from working in a community whose residents are hostile to police. In special problems, there are marked differences in social class or ethnic group makeup between the majority of community residents and the majority of department members. These have been too amply chronicled in texts and articles on police community relations to warrant detailing here.

The case of the middle- or working-class officer assigned to a lower-class neighborhood has received attention in the press and from sociologists and criminologists, but problems also exist for the officer of middle- or working-class background who works in a very wealthy community. The officers of this sort whom the authors have interviewed report having their authority questioned, being subjected to threats of political pressure, being treated as servants, and feeling that they were expected to act as baby-sitters. Certainly a routine that consists largely of service, such as checking houses of owners who are away and opening cars whose owners have locked the keys in them, is in contrast with the general perception of police as crime fighters. In these towns the major crime usually is burglary, which has notoriously low clearance rates.

Even when the community itself is not hostile to the police, it will always include some individuals who are hostile or who become so in the course of interactions with an officer. Such a person may make a very unpleasant neighbor for an officer. Just as professionals such as physicians and attorneys are often approached at social gatherings and asked for professional advice or are castigated for real or imagined failings of their profession, so, too, officers report being asked for favors by friends, neighbors, and relatives or being blamed personally for any differences of opinion his acquaintance may have had with the police. His children may be subjected to caustic comments or jokes, such as the venerable, "Does Jonah's father work? No, he's a cop."

Stressors Inherent in the Police Role

The role of the police in our society is a complex one, involving, according to Wilson (1968), three different goals: enforcing the law, maintaining order, and providing a wide range of services. Departments vary in the emphasis they put on each of these goals. Some of the stressors that impinge upon police are inherent in this role.

Society vests police with unique authority, both real and symbolic. Not only can the officer give orders and enforce them, and even deprive people of their liberty (at least for a short time), he is also the symbolic representation of everything from parent to state (Bard and Ellison, 1974). Indeed, he is one of the few authority figures who is highly visible and readily available to the general public. People tend to see him, not as an individual, but as a representative of the establishment. They hate — or love — him for what he represents. Police officers tend to overestimate public hostility. Several studies have shown that the majority of Americans feel that the police are doing a good job. The image of police is better among some groups than others: the poor, the young, and blacks give police the worst marks (Radelet, 1980).

Police officers often are in the position of being responsible for the lives and safety of others. Although most have some first aid training, again this may be minimal; yet they frequently are called upon to perform emergency procedures.

> **Case 2:1.** A command level officer in a major city tells of remembering the second baby he de-

livered. The child was born dead. Although the physician who later examined it assured him that it had died before birth, he felt guilty for weeks and kept asking himself what he might have done wrong.

Case 2:2. Detective Bill Negron was asked, as a special favor to a friend, Detective Joe LoPicio, to go with him to provide protection for his sister when she had a last confrontation with a violent boyfriend. Negron agreed, and arrangements for the encounter were made. Negron was to be behind the woman. He explained that as long as she did not go past a certain point he would be able to see and protect her. Unfortunately, she ignored these instructions and was shot to death by the boyfriend.

Negron began to drink much more heavily and felt he could not discuss his guilt feelings with anyone. He had frequent nightmares about it. Four years after the incident, he heard the senior author lecture about victimology and stress. When she said, "Victims and their families are in crisis, but there may be someone else who is in crisis, too: the police officer," he had a strong flashback and remembered all the details. The following Monday he talked with a woman detective in his office whom he knew to be a friend of the senior author, and for the first time was able to talk about his feelings.

The police work daily, furthermore, with what Wambaugh (1980) has called "the worst of people, and ordinary people at their worst." This includes people who are in crisis, people who hate the police, and criminals, some of whom have committed acts of extreme viciousness. The people who call upon the police often expect, and even demand, instant action and success.

Case 2:3. Even people who profess to dislike the police frequently come to them for help in emergencies. Stanley was one such person. A pusher, he had two charges of carrying a concealed weapon on his record. Certainly he was no friend of the police. Yet when his mother collapsed with a heart attack out-

side his favorite tavern, he did not go there and ask
his friends for help. Instead, he ran the three blocks
to the police station.

Some officers, especially those who are prone to action, have
problems adjusting to the many hours of crushing boredom that
most patrol officers endure. The boredom is made worse because of
the perception that one can never relax but must be constantly alert
and aware that around the next corner may lie a situation that involves danger or demands action. This perception is fostered in
training and in the cautionary locker room tales that tell of the doom
that befell others who relaxed their vigilance.

The officer may find conflict between two of the demands of the
goals of law enforcement, service delivery and order maintenance. A
prime example of this conflict may be seen in the question of how to
handle family fights (commonly known as domestics). The law enforcement goal demands that the officer detemine whether a crime
has been committed, or accept the complaint of an allegedly ag-
grieved party, and make an arrest. Police officers have learned, however, that the disputants frequently want only arbitration and
mediation, not arrest. Even when the immediate request is for arrest, complainants seldom follow through and may even turn on the
officer and attack him as he is making the arrest. Such a situation
suggests that order maintenance, or crisis intervention, skills are
more appropriate in this situation (Bard, 1970). Politics also enter
the arena, as women's groups have inveighed against the police for
failure to arrest in these situations.

A stressor seldom mentioned is the pension. Rather early in their
careers, officers begin to feel trapped by the pension: even though
they may no longer enjoy their work, they feel they have invested so
much in it that they cannot leave. The authors have anecdotal evidence that administrators are aware of this belief on the part of officers and realize that there is a point at which the officer will be less
likely to leave no matter how badly he is treated. Browning (1982)
believes that the practice of retirement after twenty years also lessens
officers' views of policing as a lifetime commitment; this is also
found in the military. The tendency to blame the pension for feelings
of being trapped may be a rationalization; however, few go to the
trouble of making a cost/benefit analysis of the value of the pension

compared with alternatives.

ACCIDENTAL STRESSORS. Accidental stressors come in the form of assignments that can cause crisis reactions for even the most hardened officer, including the wounding or death of a fellow officer, cases in which children have been killed or injured, disaster work, and involvement in shooting incidents. Stressors of this sort are mentioned prominently by the officers studied by Sewell (1981), Kroes and Gould (1979), and Ellison and Genz (1978).

Wambaugh dealt with the first of these stressors in *The Onion Field*. This true story details the deterioration of a conscientious officer whose partner was shot and who was publicly blamed by the department (although the circumstances were by no means clear-cut). Even in less dramatic cases, officers often travel great distances to attend the funeral of a fellow officer whom they have never met but who was killed in the line of duty. Wanted posters of suspected police killers have a prominent place in every police station remotely near the killing. In Sewell's (1981) catalogue of the events rated most stressful by FBI academy attendees and others, "violent death of a partner in the line of duty" held the first place, with a score of 88, while "violent death of another officer in the line of duty" was sixth, with a score of 79.

Many officers relate their horror in having to deal with children who have been mutilated or killed. "Answering a call to a scene involving violent nonaccidental death of a child" was rated thirteenth in Sewell's study, with a score of 70, and "response to a scene involving the accidental death of a child" was twenty-first, with a value of 68. This is one of the few occasions when officers feel free to weep openly in front of their fellows, and the one in which brutality against an offender is most likely to be condoned. The laughing and joking that relieve tension in so many other stressful situations is largely absent in these. They are frequently relived in nightmares.

Disaster work for police most frequently means handling fatal accidents. In the only available evidence of frequency of such events, Lewis (1973) found that the average officer in the Charlottesville, Virginia, police department observed a dead person approximately once every two months; presumably only some of these were accident victims. Although none of these is pleasant, it is common for officers quickly to become detached and accustomed to them (Teahan, 1975).[8]

Such detachment is less possible in accidents involving multiple casualties, such as plane crashes.[9] Awareness of the scope of the carnage overloads the senses and leads to a suspension of feeling and emotions. Some officers react to the situation with a mindless and ritualistic search for something to do, such as looking for rope to make an unrealistic barrier to prevent unauthorized persons from entering the scene. This helps them deny the helplessness they feel. Most, of course, recover swiftly from any initial chaos and perform efficiently. The chances of appropriate performance are heightened by training that includes realistic simulations or by frequent performance of such duties.

After the incident is over and the officer is relieved of duty, a common response is a breaking of the emotional dam, resulting in laughing or crying, restlessness, agitation, jumpiness, and even acting high. Similar behavior has been reported in combat troops after a battle, and in undercover agents after they have successfully completed a dangerous assignment. At times like this, most officers have a strong need to vent their emotions, usually with others who have been involved in the situation.

The need to share the experience with others who have been through this or similar incidents is found also in officers who have been involved in shooting incidents. About 100 United States officers a year kill someone in the line of duty. ("Taking a life in the line of duty" and "shooting someone in the line of duty" were third and fourth on Sewell's list.) While a few officers claim that such an incident would have no effect on them and, indeed, the authors have known some who seem to be little changed, such a response is most common in those who have not experienced it. Reactions are typical of people in crisis, with guilt and anxiety being particularly prevalent (Riede, quoted in Cohen, 1980). Michael Roberts, head of psychological services for the San Jose, California, police department, believes that virtually everyone has flashbacks of these incidents, and crying, guilt, and sorrow occur in about 25 percent of the cases (Cohen, 1980).

Further evidence of the stressfulness of taking a life in the line of duty comes from the findings of Roberts, Martin Reiser, psychologist with the LAPD, and John Stratton, who works with the Los Angeles sheriff's department. All believe that "a very high proportion of officers involved in fatal shootings ultimately leave their departments because of 'stress disability' " (Cohen, 1980). However,

> psychologists say it is impossible to predict which officers will have diffi-
> culty coping with the fact that they have killed. It depends on the cir-
> cumstances of the shooting — whether the officer or someone else was in
> imminent danger, whether he was physically close to the suspect as he
> died, his and the suspect's age, the officer's background, religious train-
> ing and a host of other factors (Cohen, 1980, p. 18).

One of these "other factors," in the authors' experience, is the identity of the deceased. It is usually easier to kill someone generally known as a hardened criminal, caught in the commission of a crime, than it is to kill a psychotic, an adolescent with what appears in a dim light to be a gun or knife but turns out to be keys, or to kill accidentally.

Also important in an officer's ability to cope with shooting incidents are the reactions of his fellow officers. They may praise him or kid him and joke with him inappropriately.

> **Case 2:4.** Investigator Charles Clark of the Middlesex County, New Jersey, prosecutor's office, frequently does internal investigations of shootings in which officers are involved. He tells of having an appointment with two officers, one of whom, in a rather complicated set of circumstances, had shot and superficially wounded a fleeing teenaged burglary suspect. At the time it was uncertain whose bullet had done the damage. Clark listened as other officers teased the two with comments such as, "Hey, Kojak! They're going to take away your sharpshooter medal." "Why didn't you waste him? Are you losing your touch?" His own comment, which was gratefully received, was, "You know, at times like this, it's all right to feel bad." This led them to admit that they had spent the evening after the shooting getting drunk together — a very common response.

A special kind of response is sometimes found in officers who have been injured on the job.[10] (The word *sometimes* must be emphasized because there is no evidence to indicate how common the syndrome is, but it is probably infrequent.) In these cases, it is not the injury itself that produces the psychological symptoms, for they are neither found in injured athletes nor in all officers who are injured.

Also, there is wide variation in the intensity and duration of the symptoms, which is not necessarily related to the seriousness of the injury. Not all the symptoms are found in every case.

After an initial period when the injured person seems to be recovering normally, he begins to become depressed and anxious, and preoccupied with the events that led up to the injury. He withdraws from family and social life. At work he is anxious, restless, and easily fatigued; concentration becomes difficult. The officer becomes increasingly irritable, tense, and hypersensitive to criticism. He develops a phobia for all kinds of police work and does not want to carry his firearm. Eventually he may become unable to work, or he may leave the department.

It should be emphasized that these symptoms are not faked. People faking trauma have no "incubation" period, they play to the audience, focusing on the pain, and they show few effects on home and social life. They are happy to take favorable limited duty assignments but resist removal of their firearms. These symptoms are most common in officers who had had good police records but who had received inadequate support at the time of the injury. The supervisor who drops by to say, "I'm sorry this happened, and we all hope you'll be back with us soon; we need and miss you," will go far toward providing this intervention.

Following is an excerpt of a newspaper article that shows the stresses of a crime scene investigation unit.

About New York
A Regimen of Man's Violence Leavened With a Bit of Humor*
By Anna Quindlen

The bedroom in the back of the apartment in Elmhurst, Queens, was small and clean, except for the dark spot on the shag carpeting. On one wall was a turquoise sombrero with gold stitching; on the other was a round, almost decorative smear of blood. There was a bed, a desk, a dresser and, in the narrow space between those three, a young man in a pair of designer jeans and a knit shirt, with small change scattered around his body. It did not take a doctor, or even a genius, to tell that he was dead.

"The ultimate indignity," said Lieut. Daniel Guiney, shaking his head.

It was difficult to tell whether the lieutenant, who is the commanding

---

*From A. Quindlen, About New York: A Regimen of Man's Violence Leavened with a Bit of Humor, *The New York Times*, August 5, 1981. © 1981 by the New York Times Company. Reprinted by permission.

officer of the Police Department's crime scene unit, meant death or law enforcement. Certainly it is bad enough to take a .45 caliber bullet through the back in a robbery that probably netted no more than a few hundred dollars. But then come the men of the crime scene unit, chronicling the minutes of violent death, edging round the victim as though he were a coffee table at a crowded cocktail party, studiously ignoring the evidence of their own mortality on the floor.

"I hope we don't miss the coffee and pastry back at the office," said Officer Charles Haase while he took crime scene photograph No. 3, a close-up of homicide victim from above.

"Me, too," said Lieutenant Guiney.

*

The 44 men of the crime scene unit photographed and examined the scenes of 184 homicides during July alone. They also worked on some suspicious suicides and pattern crimes. By the end of the year, they will have taken 60,000 pictures of places in which serious crimes were committed as well as of the crime victims. Occasionally, one of the photographers will do a wedding or sweet-16 party, to earn a little extra cash.

In a city where cleaning up after murder is an omnipresent and dirty job, they may have the dirtiest job of all, for they are at the scene of nearly every major crime. They photographed Helen Hagnes's telltale shoes on the roof of the Metropolitan Opera House and examined John Lennon's clothing for the bullet holes. When they enter a room, it is often still thick with an almost tangible miasma of violence, a palpable feeling that evil has been present there.

They fill their own offices on lower Broadway with wisecracks and smart talk, and the smell of garlic frying in olive oil. Two of the men might cook dinner for the others in the back, in the disposable plastic aprons they pick up from the morgue: baked ziti, chicken cacciatore, scampi on Friday night. "This one guy puts so much garlic in the food," said the lieutenant, "that he bent over a body one night to get a close-up and the guy woke up."

In the middle of the meal, however, the phone will ring, and dinner gives way to the big valises in which the Horseman camera and the fingerprinting kit are kept. Sometimes it will be a fairly routine call, like the one in Elmhurst, where three "perps" had entered a third-floor clothing outlet and demanded all the cash. The clerk, a Cuban refugee working two jobs, had shouted out an alarm to the owner and a customer, in the bedroom, and had tried to flee; the two other men had made it out the window, but the clerk was left, forever insensate.

"You just kind of remove yourself," said Officer Paul Chu. "I'm on the outside looking in. You have to say to yourself, 'If I were a juror, what would I want to know about how the scene looked.' You have to keep yourself uninvolved."

"I just look at it as a job, not as a person," said Officer Haase. "Except for anything involving little kids, who haven't even lived, who haven't done anything to anybody. I have kids myself."

And sometimes the men of the crime scene unit will find something useful, and that is why they like their jobs. In the Metropolitan Opera murder, they found the palm print that became a major piece of evidence against Craig Crimmins. They worked under a railroad siding, holding back their distress and disgust, when 10-year-old Lorraine Pacifico's body was discovered on Staten Island. And when they were finished with the fingerprints on a piece of beer bottle, they had found a link to the man who was arrested and charged with her murder. Sometimes it is all just like television, except that the blood is real.

When they entered the apartment in Elmhurst, they worked swiftly, with only a few wisecracks. Fingerprints were lifted for examination. An empty beer bottle and a glass were dusted on the chance that after murdering one man and wounding two, the thieves had gotten thirsty.

A man was brought up from the bedazzled mob on the street for a possible identification. He stopped and paled when he glimpsed the outstretched legs through the bedroom door. "Oh, my God," he said.

"Now this man is dead," said a precinct police officer angrily. "This man is dead and he looks dead."

"What a shame, huh?" one of the homicide detectives said to Lieutenant Guiney.

"It's always a shame," he said, disgusted. "You never get used to what people can do to other people." And as he stepped over the body in the bedroom with his men, he said: "Find me a bloody print. Find me the print the D. A. will kiss me for. Find me the prints of the guys who did this."

ESPECIALLY STRESSFUL ASSIGNMENTS. Certain assignments seem to involve high psychological risk. Those assignments in which one deals with mutilation and death, such as working in a medical examiner's office or in homicide investigation, come immediately to mind and, indeed, are stressful for many people, especially at first. However, people who work these assignments often have, or develop in the course of the work, the kind of personality that can cope with such situations (Teahan, 1975; Ward, 1979). The unpleasantness may also be ameliorated in homicide investigators by the prestige that the job holds in most departments and the respect given it by peers. Whether or not these defenses, which permit an officer to do an important job well, prevent him from doing the kind of work that involves interacting with others is a question open to research. For analogy, some evidence in the medical literature shows that surgeons learn to harden themselves and think of patients as organs rather than as people. This seldom leads to a good bedside manner.

As long as a job requires only one basic skill or personality, problems may be minimized. Special problems may arise in assignments that require varied, contradictory skills and defenses. Many tasks in policing require human interaction skills, the kind in which it is impossible to follow a formula. These are the tasks which require a different response to each situation and from different individuals.

When the necessity for interaction and sensitivity to human feelings and behavior is combined in an assignment with the necessity for dealing with situations that demand distancing because they incur basic human fears of mutilation, trauma, and death, the officer must attempt to perform the balancing act of working appropriately with clients who are undergoing ego-threatening crises and at the same time of protecting his own ego. Respondents in an unpublished survey that the authors conducted listed several assignments that fit in the category of being particularly stressful: undercover work, particularly in narcotics, sex crimes investigation, and, increasingly, juvenile work.

Undercover narcotics provides an interesting vehicle for a look at a particularly stressful assignment.[11] The officer's success, and survival, depend on his ability to blend with what can only be acknowledged as some of the least wholesome elements of society. He must learn to talk, to act, even try to think as they do. (One officer we know reached the point, after six years of undercover work, that she would not turn around if a friend called to her on the street using her real name. She responded only to her street name.) Most report that it is not easy to keep the two identities separate; as one said, "When you live with scum constantly, it is hard not to get covered with it." (Many narcotics officers, however, take pride in their ability to separate the two worlds and resent comments that suggest they may have succumbed to the temptation to try illicit drugs.)

Stress reactions and burnout also are seen more frequently in patrol officers who must handle large numbers of calls that involve serious problems which they are not equipped by training or mandate to solve. Residents of urban ghettos commonly call the police with such problems (Muir, 1977; Bard, 1974). Lacking access to other sources of service, poor people use the police as psychologist, plumber, ambulance, arbitrator, ombudsman with other public agencies, child disciplinarian, and even, occasionally, baby-sitter. The hypothesis that such officers would be more prone to burnout is

consistent with the finding by Maslach (1976) with other professionals that "burnout often becomes inevitable when the professional
is forced to provide care for too many people. As the ratio increases,
the result is higher and higher emotional overload until, like a wire
that has too much electricity flowing through it, the worker just
burns out and emotionally disconnects."

Stressors in the Organizational Structure and in Supervisory Style

An important, often neglected, source of stress in policing is
found in the structure of the organization and in supervisory style.[12]
Virtually all the stress management programs for police officers discussed in the literature focus on the individual (Blackmore, 1978;
Terry, 1981).[13] Yet, as has already been noted, many studies of police
stress have identified organizational variables as major sources of
pressure (Kroes, 1976; Hillgren, Bond, and Jones, 1976; Stotland,
1975; Aldang and Brief, 1978; Ellison and Genz, 1978). This is, in
fact, the most parsimonious explanation for the large differences in
morale and other indicators of pressure found among departments.
Job stress, then, is exacerbated and indeed may be caused by certain
practices that are common in police organizations but, as innovative
programs have shown, are not necessary parts of the police role.

One of the more devastating of these traditional practices is the
indiscriminate use of the military model, which sees police tasks as
technological ones. It assumes that every assignment involves skills
that do not vary greatly from individual to individual or from setting
to setting. It views discretion as unimportant and inappropriate for
all but high level supervisors.

Certainly there are skills and assignments in policing for which
such a model is appropriate and necessary — assignments such as
riot duty approximate combat conditions — but for many others it is
not. Many, if not most, police tasks involve managing people. Individuals may accomplish these tasks differently, depending on personality style, size and appearance, sex, and the like. For example, a
small person may handle a bar brawl differently from a large one,
and a male officer may use different techniques in interviewing a
child than would a female, although all can find strategies to accomplish the job.

Furthermore, unlike the combat soldier, who lives and fights in the company of a large group of others doing approximately the same job, the police officer usually works alone or with a single partner. He is continually called upon to exercise discretion (Skolnick, 1966; Wilson, 1968; Hillgren, Bond, and Jones, 1976). Untrained in its exercise, told that it is not part of his job and that it is inappropriate for one of his rank (Hillgren, Bond, and Jones, 1976), seldom rewarded for the many instances when he exercises judgment appropriately, but often punished if actions attract adverse public attention, the creative person learns to take the conservative path, not to make waves, and to go by the book even when such action may be damaging to his larger mandate to serve and protect.

In contrast, recent research indicates that the more autonomy police officers possess, the more satisfied they are with their work (Greenberg and Smith, 1979; Stotland, 1975). This is consistent with studies in the literature of organizational psychology that show that participatory management styles increase not only workers' satisfaction but also their commitment to organizational goals (Fiedler, 1967; Hampton, Summer, and Webber, 1978).

Stotland (1975) sees negative consequences in another facet of the military model: the use of a strict pyramid-shaped hierarchical structure, based on military ranks. He believes this structure decreases the sense of professionalism of those at the bottom of the pyramid, particularly patrolmen, leading to lowered self-esteem. Having many ranks, director, chief, deputy chiefs, inspectors, majors, captains, lieutenants, sergeants, corporals, and patrolmen, increases the social distance between the top and the bottom, bringing an "aura of intrinsic status differences — differences in the very quality of the human beings involved" (p. 13), which also damage morale. Once it is established in a department, unfortunately, the military model is difficult to change.[14]

A corollary of the military model is the view of the police officer as a Renaissance man. Once the officer pins on his badge, some departments seem to believe he is magically able to perform any task to which he may be assigned, regardless of training, interest, experience, or personality style. As one supervisor in a survey (Ellison and Genz, 1976) said to a man given a clerical assignment who complained that he did not know how to type, "You've got ten fingers; of course you can type."

Role conflict and role ambiguity, found to be stressful in other jobs (see Chapter 1), also are found in some police organizations. Aldang and Brief (1978), in one of the few studies that specifically measures these variables in police, found that officers who felt little role ambiguity were highly motivated, felt satisfied with their work, and were committed to the organization. Knowing what was expected of them and having a sense of mutual trust with supervisors was particularly important. This is consistent with the findings of Kroes and Gould (1979) and others that officers find a lack of administrative support particularly frustrating. Role conflict can also come from the situation mentioned earlier in which demands of the three basic functions of police, law enforcement, peacekeeping, and provision of service, are in conflict.

The authors' impression is that may departments have regulations that are ambiguous or conflicting, which are formulated in response to some crisis rather than as part of a systematic development of policy and which are seldom reviewed or culled. Thus, some rule or interpretation can be found to condemn any action. This is a special problem in departments that try to make rules to cover every possible contingency. The right approach often depends on the situation, which returns to the exercise of discretion. This idea also has received anecdotal support from Daviss (1982).

As Terry (1981) points out, supervisory styles are only partially able to deal with role conflicts and ambiguities. This may be in part because the supervisors themselves often feel these pressures and have a limited sense of control. Hillgren, Bond, and Jones (1976) found sentiments of this sort in a study of police chief administrators. Just as patrol officers often felt that administrators gave them no support and that success depended on political whim within the police organization, so, too, administrators felt their jobs were greatly hampered by lack of backing from the officials to whom they reported.

> It is not surprising that few attempts have been successful in reducing the amount of stress experienced by police officers. A common characteristic of many of these stressors is lack of administrative backing which in turn is often due to the influence of politics upon the administration. These politics are defined broadly as "The conflict over the goals and personnel of government" and underlie many of the stressors affecting chief administrators. If a chief, for example, were to provide the necessary support to his personnel for using discretion in ambiguous situations, the result could be a dissatisfied influential citizen or citizens

group. Consequently, the citizenry, the press, and city officials would
question the chief administrator's competency in supporting the use of
such discretion by his officers. Understandably, an administrator is reluctant to offer such backing when he has little support, and he may
even be penalized for doing so (p. 447).

As budgets are becoming tighter and as resources are cut, overload is becoming more important, even in departments that previously have had the luxury of providing a wide variety of special
services and responding promptly to every call. In these situations it
is particularly important that the department set priorities. Few in
law enforcement have been willing to acknowledge that the days of
seemingly limitless federal funds may be over. There is much complaining that it is impossible to do the task with available resources.
The authors are less pessimistic, believing that perhaps the task cannot be done the same way with fewer resources, but that alternatives
may exist. In crime prevention, for example, the police seem to be
acknowledging that they alone can have little impact and are focusing efforts on support of citizens' groups such as crime watch programs.

An important part of the strain that comes from organizational
or supervisory styles is the individual's perception of a lack of control
over his working conditions. This happens when requests for assignments to, or removal from, certain jobs are repeatedly ignored and
when an officer believes that rewards come from who he knows and
not how he performs. It is made worse by lack of consistent feedback
about performance or workable suggestions for improvement. Often, lower ranking officers develop a perception of "us" versus
"them" within the department: the belief, described earlier, that
bosses and workers are on different sides. This stance is, unfortunately, frequently furthered by rhetoric from bargaining units.

Contributing to the stress caused by lack of control over one's
working conditions is the paradox that, in the exercise of his duties,
the officer, by his mandate, has enormous control over the lives of
others. He can detain and question them and deprive them of their
liberty or even of their lives. To many, this stands in stark contrast
with their lack of control over their own lives. For example, in most
departments in which the authors have worked, officers have limited
say about their shifts or assignments. In some departments, an officer who calls in sick must be instantly available to phone and house

checks by a police surgeon. If he goes to the pharmacy to fill a prescription, he is put on report and is subject to disciplinary action.

No discussion of the stressors in organizational structure can ignore the issue of shift work. Research has shown consistently that rotating shifts, especially those that rotate on a weekly basis, have an adverse effect on physical condition and on one's ability to work at maximum efficiency (Folkard and Monk, 1979; Meers, Maasen, and Verhaagen, 1978). This is a particular problem, of course, when a job requires good reflexes and the ability to make quick judgments.

One study of twenty-one Wisconsin departments, some of which were on fixed and some on rotating shifts, found that, while 46 percent enjoyed shift work and 47 percent accepted it as a condition of employment, 83 percent of the officers preferred a permanent shift schedule. Fifty-seven percent preferred the day shift, 21 percent the afternoon shift, and 19 percent liked nights. The respondents in this study felt the greatest effect on their family lives (49%) (Brunner, 1976). In a study of Newark police officers, who rotate shifts weekly, Engler (1980) found that 75 percent of the men would prefer steady shifts, while only 5 percent wanted to continue the present schedule. Seventy-four percent of the men were dissatisfied with their eating habits, and 64 percent experienced sleeping disorders. In addition, 91 percent of the wives disliked the rotating schedule.

Despite the weight of the evidence against rotating shifts, it is still common practice in the police departments with which the authors are acquainted. One of the worst work schedules has fallen to a friend of the junior author: he works 4PM to midnight on Tuesday and Wednesday, midnight to 8AM Thursday and Friday, and 8AM to 4PM on Saturday. He has had this schedule for fifteen years.

Indicators of stress due to organizational style include such gauges of low morale as absenteeism, sabotage of group goals, high turnover, and a department constantly in turmoil over rumors.

Individual Personalities

Personality factors in coping have received by far the most attention from social science researchers and police administrators. Personal variables that have been studied include general psychological functioning, measured by standard personality tests (Spielberger,

1979), special coping styles (Diskin, Goldstein, and Grencik, 1977), past history of coping, and other events that have taken place in one's life (Lefkowitz, 1977). Such emphasis leads to solutions involving better selection procedures and in-service screening to weed out the "inadequate" personality. It also makes the assumption that there is an ideal police personality (Lefkowitz, 1977).

Levy (1967) has criticized the screening approach on several grounds, pointing out that

> (a) the mere absence of unwanted qualities before employment has not necessarily indicated a continuation of such absence after employment;
> (b) we have not determined what constitutes "emotional suitability" for law enforcement; hence,
> (c) psychological tests and psychiatric interviews have not demonstrated much predictive value; and
> (d) the assumption that psychological problems lower the tolerance to stress is a limited one.

Rhead and his colleagues (1968) add that "certain traits ordinarily considered to be 'pathological' are essential ingredients of the personality structure of the 'normal' police officer" (p. 1577). The essence of this comment is that the psychiatrist or clinical psychologist may have a rather narrow view of what is normal, seeing it in terms of the middle-class male (Broverman et al., 1970). It is possible that someone with such a personality might have trouble surviving as a police officer on the streets of a large city and that the definition of "normal" should be reexamined.

Studies that attempt to predict job success by specific operational criteria have been more successful than the traditional psychiatric screening techniques. They seem to show that

> the "successful" policeman is more likely than his less successful colleague to be of high measured intelligence and to perform well on civil service exams and in recruit training. He presents a more stable previous work history, usually in a skilled occupation, and his early family history, present life-style, and family life also present a highly stable and conventional picture, devoid of mobility or impulsiveness. Dominant features of his personality include a sense of independence, self-assurance, little need for external ego supports, high energy and good health, and well-balanced impulse control — that is, he presents an overall picture of being emotionally well-adjusted (Lefkowitz, 1977, p. 357).[15]

Little research has been conducted on the cognitive styles, discussed in Chapter 1, that are thought to exacerbate or ameliorate stress in police. Indirect evidence does come from the work of Novaco (1977), who has trained officers to deal with anger by changing their ways of thinking about potentially provocative situations. This work will be described more fully in Chapter 6.

There should, nevertheless, be certain minimum requirements for police officers in all jurisdictions, including average intelligence and the ability to read and write, as well as the absence of major physical and psychological disabilities. Beyond these very general factors, the appropriate characteristics for officers may vary from jurisdiction to jurisdiction and from assignment to assignment within a department. To determine the appropriate characteristics for a particular department or assignment, one should employ the tools of the industrial psychologist rather than those of the clinician. Of these tools, the most important is the job analysis.[16] Of course, civil service and civil rights restrictions may limit flexibility in personnel decisions.

Identifying the personality type best suited to perform competently under good conditions and recruiting people who fit this type is not a guarantee of success, however. Personalities change; indeed, Skolnick (1967) has described at length the development of the officer's "working personality." As Levy (1967) implied, even the best, healthiest, most dedicated officer may succumb to stress if external pressures are great enough. Some of the insulating qualities that make for resistance to burnout and that could be used as a basis for selection are in fact undesirable for other reasons. For example, people with rigid personalities suffer less role conflict than those who are more flexible, but rigidity of behavior is not an asset in jobs where discretion plays an important part. The psychopath is also less likely to feel the pressures, but he is most likely to end up with corruption charges.

Special Problems: Female and Minority Group Officers

Police officers, generally known as a tightly knit group, tend to resent the intrusion of outsiders (Broderick, 1977). Members of "out" groups who have tried to gain entry into policing frequently report hostility and resentment from white male officers (Alex, 1969; Milton, 1972; Martin, 1980).

One study of policewomen summarized the problems they face as follows:

> The difficulties that policewomen were found to face in entering a traditionally male occupation emanate from structural features of the work organization and cultural features governing male-female interaction. Departmental policies often put the policewomen at a disadvantage by failing to meet their unique needs and permitting the development of a cycle of demotivation and failure on the part of some women. The policemen's working subculture, built on mutual trust of officers with similar backgrounds, attitudes, and values, is threatened by the presence of policewomen. For this reason, women are not accepted as officers and are frequently denied information, alliances, protection, and sponsorship necessary for success in the department's formal and informal structure.
>
> At the interpersonal level, female officers must contend with the strains of status inferiority as women, compounded by performance pressures as tokens present in limited numbers. They are cast into limited stereotypic roles and pressured by male peers to remain subordinate through a variety of verbal and nonverbal cues.
>
> Policewomen adopt two patterns of behavior as a result of the dilemmas they face: one group succeeds as officers by a strategy of overachievement, invisibility, and strict adherence to the rules, while the other adapts to the stereotypic roles into which women are cast, remaining "ladies" and being less successful as patrol officers (Martin, 1977).

Officers who are members of racial minority groups also are often denied access to the informal channels of support and information that are an important part of police work. In addition, they cite frequent incidents of racial slurs and ostracism, both from fellow officers and from members of their own racial groups whom they confront in the course of their work. This problem is particularly acute in departments that have few minority group officers.

Although the general problems encountered by minority group members and women who join police forces have received some attention, there is little specific research on differences in stress-related disorders, either between white male officers and members of other groups or between minority group officers and members of that group who hold other jobs. In one such effort, Silbert (1982), in her study of new officers in San Francisco, found that the women were slightly more stressed by police work than the men and had slightly higher burnout scores. They felt more jittery, more physically exhausted, and more irritated than men and had significantly more headaches and backaches, as well as more stomachaches and problems sleeping. This finding may be in part due to the well-documented tendency of women to be more willing than men to report illness. Black officers reported the lowest stress as a result of policing frustrations, and Latin officers reported the highest stress.

Influence of the Family

The family can be a major source of support in mediating stress reactions. It is logical, as a result, that studies of the family would be of special concern and importance in stress research. Many research questions come to mind. First, what is the direction of the influence? Does the family serve as a source of support, buffering against the stressors of a job, or does disruption in the family decrease job efficiency? Do job pressures carry over into personal life so that a worker with a very stressful job is likely to carry the pressures home and take his frustrations out on his family? Is the family, as Handy (1981) queries, help or hindrance? Surprisingly, the number of studies is small; more is known about the families of police than of other occupational groups, and comparisons are rare indeed.

Policemen, Bayley and Mendelsohn (1969) tell us, are family men; they are also parents. This makes a study of the impact of the job on the family, and vice versa, particularly salient.

Much of what passes for literature on the impact of family life on police officers consists of anecdotal accounts by officers' wives (Prunier, 1979; James and Nelson, 1975; Webber, 1974). These tend to be of the "I'll stand by my man," although "nobody knows the trouble I've seen" variety. Indeed, both officers and their wives believe that the police marriage is uniquely stressful and prone to divorce (Niederhoffer and Niederhoffer, 1978; Kroes, Margolis, and Hurrell, 1974). The blame, incidentally, is usually placed on the wife, who is expected to make the home a haven, with her own needs pushed into the background (Webber, 1974; James and Nelson, 1975), very much in the mold of the *Total Woman* (Morgan, 1975).

Some research data support these anecdotal reports (Ward, 1979; Hurrell and Kroes, 1975; Hageman, 1978; Eisenberg, 1975). Blackmore (1978) reports that 37 percent of the officers in his massive study of twenty-nine departments had serious marital difficulties. Danto (1978) claims that marital problems are the single most important precipitating stress factor in police suicides, and Kroes,

Margolis, and Hurrell (1974) and Hillgren, Bond, and Jones (1976) report that married police administrators believed that the work affected their home lives. They complained of the loss of nonpolice friends and the effects of the job on their social life in general. Rotating shifts were held to be particularly detrimental (Niederhoffer and Niederhoffer, 1978). Other complaints centered on the psychological fears of injury and on social stigma (Kroes, 1976).

Maynard, Maynard, McCubbin, and Shao (1980) found that wives of officers in "a large metropolitan police department in the Midwest" used a variety of strategies to cope with the impact of the job on family life. The development of self-reliance and assertiveness were found to be particularly important. Many of the wives surveyed by the Niederhoffers also stated that they had found positive ways of coping.

A major flaw with most of these studies is the lack of comparison with other occupations or the comparison with occupations such as physician (Niederhoffer and Niederhoffer, 1978), which are inappropriate. Because the literature on the sociology of the family almost universally supports the importance of social class in determining patterns of family interaction — and because of the debate over whether policing is a profession (Broderick, 1977) — use of an occupation that draws, as policing does, primarily from the children of the working class would seem more appropriate as a comparison group than physicians.

The data about the incidence of divorce are most likely to yield comparisons with other occupations; however, information on divorce among police is contradictory, and many of the studies are poorly done (Terry, 1981). Some studies seem to show that police divorce rates are higher than the national average (Blackmore, 1978; Baxter, 1978; Durner, Kroeker, Miller, and Reynolds, 1975; Skolnick, 1966); others present lower rates (Terry, 1981; Niederhoffer and Niederhoffer, 1978). In particular, some departments have much higher rates than others, so divorce may be one indicator of the importance of management style on stress reactions. On the whole, Terry (1981, p. 68) concludes that "the best evidence available supports the argument that police divorce rates are lower than the popular depiction of police family life would lead one to anticipate," a finding that echoes Niederhoffer and Niederhoffer's (1978) excellent review of the literature.

The preceding studies of family problems have focused on police-*men*. The work on police*women* shows that, although they have extremely high divorce rates, most of these divorces occurred prior to the woman's entry into the force (Niederhoffer and Niederhoffer, 1978), and there is no evidence that the authority vested in a police officer follows the policewoman into the home in the same way it is said to follow the policeman. When she takes off the uniform, she tends to assume a rather traditional wifely role. Also, while most policemen tell their wives little about the job, disclosures of this sort by policewomen to their husbands is common. This may also be due in part to the possibility that some of these policewomen are married to policemen. Although the authors know many such couples, they have no information on their prevalence.

Other indicators of family problems have received much less attention. There is little work on the incidence of spouse or child abuse or of special problems displayed by the children of officers. Officers and their wives frequently complain about the effect of the rotating shift on interaction with children, but the Niederhoffers point out that

> In the larger cities, police department hours of work, time off, and vacations compare quite favorably with those of other civil service workers and most of the working force in the private sector as well. . . . by judiciously manipulating his periods of sleep, a police officer on rotating shifts can enjoy far more of the day with his children than does the average working father with regular hours. He can also see his children at different times during the day, an especially rewarding benefit when the children are small and have early bedtimes. Compared with a busy professional or the harried middle-class executive who brings his work home with him almost every night, the police officer enjoys a great advantage (pp. 150 – 151).

Rumors of infidelity are rampant in every police organization with which the authors have come in contact. One police psychologist (Smith, 1982) reports that many officers he counsels admit to it, and police chaplains consider it a serious problem (Niederhoffer and Niederhoffer, 1978). However, there are no data to show how common it is or whether it is more common among officers than in other occupations. It may be that, like divorce or the actual physical danger of the job, expectations outweigh the reality.

If the family is indeed affected by the job, does the harmony or disharmony of the family also influence the officer's ability to perform at work? Even less research asks this question. The possibility that it may be so underlies the establishment of programs for police families. Wives, in addition, often believe the department should help the family. Surveys indicate that they would like departments to provide them with a variety of services (Niederhoffer and Niederhoffer, 1978), including family or marital counseling, orientation programs for wives, and social activities. The substantial number of wives who wanted no services at all "made it clear that the fear of departmental intrusion into their private lives overrode their desire for help" (p. 131).

Some departments — 40 percent of the ninety-four surveyed by the Niederhoffers — have responded to these needs. Their programs include courses for wives (and sometimes financées and mothers) that range from brief orientation sessions to courses that last several weeks (Hightshoe and Hightshoe, 1978; Maynard and Maynard, 1980; Saper, 1980; Stratton, 1978; Leyden, 1977; Megerson, 1976). Content includes everything from information about police work to firearms training to "couples communication training." Some departments permit spouses to ride along with police officers to get a first-hand look at the job (Leyden, 1977). More comprehensive services, such as counseling, are less common and may be provided by the police chaplain (Niederhoffer and Niederhoffer, 1978) or through referrals to outside agencies.

As with other training programs, there is little evidence on the effect of such courses on indicators of pressures, for example, divorce. At the most, they report that participants were enthusiastic about the course.

Much more study of the complex interaction between stressors and buffers from police work and from the family is needed. Such work would give a stronger theoretical basis for programs of reciprocal support between the two institutions.

Summary

There is general agreement that policing has the potential to be stressful. Some of the pressures police officers encounter come from external sources; thus, they are beyond the control of anyone in the department. Others suggest changes in the organizational structures or supervisory styles, while still others require effort on the part of the individual officer. In most cases, change should come at several levels.[17]

Whether policing is more stressful than other occupations remains a question for research. Data are difficult to come by, and other varibles such as sedentary work habits, social class, or even diet may have more of an impact on stress levels than the nature of the job itself (Terry, 1981).

Another problem inherent in any discussion of stress in policing is that of the potential for a self-fulfilling prophecy. We know all too well that the expectation of problems can initiate them. Terry (1981) sums it up in the following way:

> Regardless by whom this topic is discussed analytically, many police officers have given their lives in pursuance of their work, particularly in large urban areas where the crime problem is the greatest. This is indeed regretable. If police work is to get a better handle on this problem, it must not view its task as more stressful and/or dangerous than it is, for to do so is to heighten the "symbolic assailant," which every police officer must guard against (p. 70)[18] [references deleted].

Despite the seeming enormity of the task, good policing is possible. Efforts at stress management, it is hoped, will be one step toward that goal.

NOTES

1. The FBI National Academy offers advanced in-service training for officers from around the country; attendance is generally considered a privilege. It is not a recruit training program.

2. Figures of this kind may be affected by policies about sick leave, of course, and may reflect this as much as actual illnesses.

3. Laborers are much more likely than police officers to be victims of homicide; however, this can scarcely be considered a consequence of the occupation.

4. Terry (1981) suggests that these data seem to indicate that police suicide rates are linked to social class membership and a subculture of violence as much as to the specific pressures of the job.

5. Kroes fails to identify either the department or his source.

6. Other authors, such as Kroes (1976) and Hillgren, Bond, Jones (1976), use somewhat different classification schemes. The authors will include their items in the categories they have chosen to

use presently.

7. The evidence seems to show that both are right in some ways. Few cases ever go to trial; they are, instead, lost for a variety of reasons or result in plea bargaining. However, those that do go to trial are very likely to result in conviction (Ellison and Buckhout, 1981).

8. For a more detailed discussion of this process, see Terry (1981).

9. This discussion draws on unpublished work by Martin Symonds, a psychiatrist who has worked for many years with the New York City police department and who was himself once an officer.

10. This section draws on a lecture by Symonds, "Psychological Responses to Injury in Police Officers," presented at a symposium, *Police Mental Health*, held at John Jay College in New York, June 1979.

11. In his twenty-five years of police work, the junior author has worked closely with, and supervised, officers holding undercover assignments, including narcotics.

12. This contrasts with the bulk of the literature on policing, which focuses on the socialization process (Lefkowitz, 1977). One explanation for the difference might be that the bulk of the literature on policing in general is the work of sociologists, while clinical psychologists are prominent in the police stress field.

13. The authors immodestly note that the programs they have conducted are an exception (see Ellison and Genz, 1978; Ellison, Cross, and Genz, 1980).

14. For a lucid discussion of the reasons the military model was originally adopted, its strengths and weaknesses, and the models that have superseded it in some departments see Broderick (1977).

15. A complete discussion of problems in police selection is beyond the scope of this book. The interested reader is referred to Lefkowitz (1977) for a critical appraisal and to Spielberger (1977) for specifics of various programs.

16. For references to the use of job analyses in policing, see Lefkowitz (1977).

17. For further discussions of the problems of trying to implement change in policing, see Lefkowitz (1977) and Broderick (1977).

18. "Symbolic assailants" are people who "use gesture, language, and attire that the policeman has come to recognize as a pre-

lude to violence. This does not mean that violence by the symbolic assailant is necessarily predictable. On the contrary, the policeman responds to the vague indication of danger suggested by appearance" (Skolnick, 1967).

Chapter 3

RECOGNIZING STRESS REACTIONS

Introduction

THIS chapter will present more specifically some of the instruments and lists of variables, both stressors and reactions, that have been used to study stress. In contrast with the first two chapters, this and the chapters that follow will present less research data and be more speculative and more informal. They aim to provoke thought and, perhaps, to give guidance to the police administrator or officer concerned with the possibility of stress-related problems, either in his department or in his own life.

Before beginning the catalogue of events that may be stressful and behaviors that may indicate that an individual is under pressure, the authors wish to submit a few words of caution. As mentioned earlier, taking tests that may indicate problems carries with it the risk of setting up a self-fulfilling prophecy, which can lead to despair and hopelessness. One can come to feel overwhelmed by the magnitude of problems and become incapable of action. Certainly that is not the authors' aim.

People differ in their reactions to events generally considered stressful; there are differences both from one person to another and, for an individual, from one time in his life to another. Indeed, some people thrive on pressure and change. Here, as elsewhere, it is impossible to give hard and fast rules. There are, however, some commonly observed reactions in people who feel pressured and in events that most people find stressful. Certain behaviors or changes in behavior *may* signal that stress is beginning to overwhelm an individual. The word may is emphasized, because supervisors and friends must avoid the temptation to play amateur analyst and jump too quickly to conclusions. This does not mean that such signs should be ignored, however. The wisest course is to check out hunches cautiously, with a professional, if necessary, rather than to err either in assuming a problem exists when none does, and taking action that may bring on the problem one is trying to prevent, or in assuming that everything is fine, ignoring what could turn into a serious problem.

A final caveat is that, while the stressors and symptoms discussed here are individual ones, the cause may rest outside the individual, in one or a combination of those factors described earlier: organizational style, political climate, and the like. This is particularly likely when problems indicative of low morale are found in many members of a department. Suggestions for dealing with problems of this sort will be found in Chapter 4.

Two elements of behavior tend to indicate a continuing problem rather than a mild, transient reaction. Behavior — or change in behavior — that tends to be excessive, especially in comparison to that of others doing the same job, and that is prolonged is evidence of a problem. (An occasional bad day, or even several bad months in response to a specific, identifiable stressor, such as a death in the family, is no cause for alarm.)

Recognizing Stress Reactions in Others

Changes brought on by pressure may affect many areas of an individual's functioning. In fact they frequently affect several at the same time, including general changes in temperament and personality, changes in physical appearance and in health, and changes in work patterns.[1]

PERSONALITY CHANGES. Personality changes may come at both ends of the spectrum. Thus, both agitation and depression have been described as stress symptoms.

Depression manifests itself in expressions of remorse, self-pity, guilt, insecurity, loss of self-confidence, hopelessness, and despair. The officer may talk of giving up or of quitting the job. He withdraws from social contacts, and even from family members. The authors have known several officers who tell of coming home from work emotionally exhausted, sitting in a chair with a whiskey bottle, turning on the television to the station to which it was already set, and watching with no idea of what was happening. It is not uncommon for people who are having problems in living to vacillate rapidly between unusual highs and periods of deep depression.

A symptom of depression that deserves special comment is talk of committing suicide. Often this is done at first in an almost joking manner, but such talk should always be taken very seriously. Also, it is not uncommon for a person contemplating suicide to be obviously upset and agitated for some time and then to become calm. Others may believe that the problems have blown over; professionals warn that this is a particularly dangerous time, when the person's mind has been made up.[2]

Agitation is part of the disorder commonly known as mania. The symptoms of agitation include what psychologists call inappropriate affect, with the officer always on "cloud nine," even in the most difficult and tension-filled circumstances. Ceaselessly active, they seem tireless. Manic and depressive phases may alternate.

Problems may be indicated when a mild-mannered, reasonably sociable and even-tempered officer becomes aggressive, irritable, and unreasonable. He may explode at supervisors, fellow officers, friends, and/or citizens with little justification. He may talk incessantly about being persecuted by one or many others: the chief hates him, the mayor's brother has it in for him, all civilians are out to keep him from doing his job, and the like. Of course, some of what may at first appear as paranoid may have a basis in reality. Indeed, some superiors do have favorites and scapegoats. This "kernel of truth" is what makes it so difficult to differentiate between reality and paranoia.

Finally, changes in dependence on drugs, whether mood alterers, such as tranquilizers and antidepressants, or alcohol, or such everyday drugs as aspirin and antacids, may indicate problems. (In one department with which the authors work, aspirin is called "police popcorn.") When the officer who had an occasional drink after work now closes down several bars each day, a supervisor or friend may have cause for concern.

PHYSICAL CHANGES. The diseases that have been associated with stress are enumerated in Chapter 1. Other physical symptoms include the following:

1. Sudden, inappropriate gain or loss of weight
2. Complaints about physical problems and frequent "minor" ailments
3. Chest pains when the doctor can find nothing wrong (This may be an acute anxiety attack.)[3]
4. Chronic tiredness, lethargy, insomnia
5. Trembling hands or facial tics
6. Sudden concern for physical condition: a passion for weight lifting, running, and the like.

A final set of physical changes that may indicate stress-related problems is in grooming. The ordinarily well-groomed officer becomes sloppy, loses interest in his appearance, and frequently comes to work unshaven, with his hair untidy and his uniform soiled and wrinkled (as if he had spent the night in his car, as, indeed, he may have). At the other extreme, a normally more casual officer may develop a "Marine Corps footlocker" approach.

CHANGES IN WORK PATTERNS. Changes in work patterns may be seen in an officer who normally handles difficult situations calmly and efficiently who begins to let these situations get out of control. He may have a great increase in physical involvement with citizens, including numerous arrests for the most trivial offenses that could have been avoided and increases in charges of resisting arrest. Numerous civilian complaints of discourtesy or abuse may also be noticed.[4]

Dramatic changes in activity, such as a substantial increase in moonlighting or a dramatic increase in arrests, especially end of tour arrests that always result in overtime, are often symptoms of financial problems. Other problems at home may lead to sleeping at the station rather than at home, or calls from the spouse to discuss problems. One problem that spouses may call about which is a particular problem is the charge of physical assault.

Another change in activity that often is serious is when the officer rides the fine line between bravery and recklessness in serious confrontations. He may develop a "don't give a damn" attitude.

Any number of pressures may lead to frequent requests to be excused from work on short notice, frequent short absences, chronic lateness (especially in an officer who is ordinarily punctual), and abuse of sick leave.

While the appearance of such symptoms may indicate that a person is suffering from pressure that he is not dealing with well from some source, it is difficult to know just what the problem is from the behavior. For example, chronic lateness may be the result of a drinking problem, marital difficulties, unhappiness with an assignment, or a number of other woes.

Inferences from Stressful Events

As mentioned in Chapter 1, certain events are stressful to almost everyone, and some researchers believe that smaller pressures can add up to create trouble. The Stressful Life Events Scale created by Holmes and his colleagues is shown in Table 3-I. These authors (Holmes and Rahe, 1967; Holmes and Masuda, 1974) found evidence that changes in one's life totalling more than 300 life change units (LCU) within one year led to an increased risk of physical or psychological disorders within the next two years. (For a critical evaluation of this scale, reread Chapter 1.)

Table 3-I

STRESSFUL LIFE EVENTS SCALE

Life Event	LCU Value
Death of spouse	100
Divorce	73
Marital separation	65
Jail term	63
Death of close family member	63
Personal injury or illness	53
Marriage	50
Fired from work	47
Marital reconciliation	45
Retirement	45
Change in family member's health	44
Pregnancy	40
Sex difficulties	39
Gain of new family member	39
Business readjustment	39

Life Event	LCU Value
Change in financial state	38
Death of close friend	37
Career change	36
Change in number of arguments with spouse	35
Mortgage over $10,000*	31
Foreclosure of mortgage or loan	30
Change in responsibilities at work	29
Son or daughter leaving home	29
Trouble with in-laws	29
Outstanding personal achievement	28
Spouse begins or stops work	26
Starting or finishing school	26
Change in living conditions	25
Revision of personal habits	24
Trouble with boss	23
Change in work hours or conditions	20
Change in residence	20
Change in schools	20
Change in recreation habits	19
Change in church activities	19
Change in social activities	19
Mortgage or loan less than $10,000*	17
Change in sleeping habits	16
Change in number of family gatherings	15
Change in eating habits	15
Vacation	13
Christmas season	12
Minor violation of the law	11

SOURCE: T.H. Holmes and R.H. Rahe, The Social Readjustment Rating Scale, *Journal of Psychosomatic Medicine*, *11*:213-218, 1967. Reprinted by permission.

*In considering the importance of this item, it might be well to take into account that the scale was developed in the 1960s; today perhaps the value should be altered to account for inflation.

Criticism has been leveled at the Holmes and Rahe scale because it does not take into account individual differences in perceiving a given event as stressful. Sarason (1981) presents one alternative to the use of standardized weights (such as "Death of spouse" = 100). He uses the following instructions:

Listed below are a number of events which may bring about changes in the lives of those who experience them. Rate each event that occurred in your life during the past year in the following three ways:
1. Was the event Good or Bad?
2. How much did the event affect your life?
(Rated from "No Effect" to "Great Effect.")

3. To what extent did you have control over the event's occurrence? (Rated from "Not at All" to "Completely.")

He also added a number of items not found in the Holmes and Rahe listing. Although much less work has been done using this scale (or any of the other alternatives that have been proposed) than the Holmes and Rahe scale, and the evidence on relationship to problems is much more tenuous, that is, the "danger" score is not presented so specifically, which may be an advantage, subjects and people testing themselves are less likely to argue with it.

Other stressors are unique to policing. Those that Sewell's study found most stressful may be found in Table 3-II.

Table 3-II
25 MOST STRESSFUL LAW ENFORCEMENT CRITICAL LIFE EVENTS

1. Violent death of a partner in the line of duty.
2. Dismissal.
3. Taking a life in the line of duty.
4. Shooting someone in the line of duty.
5. Suicide of an officer who is a close friend.
6. Violent death of another officer in the line of duty.
7. Murder committed by a police officer.
8. Duty-related violent injury (shooting).
9. Violent job-related injury to another officer.
10. Suspension.
11. Passed over for promotion.
12. Pursuit of an armed suspect.
13. Answering a call to a scene involving violent nonaccidental death of a child.
14. Assignment away from family for a long period of time.
15. Personal involvement in a shooting incident.
16. Reduction in pay.
17. Observing an act of police corruption.
18. Accepting a bribe.
19. Participating in an act of police corruption.
20. Hostage situation resulting from aborted criminal action.
21. Response to a scene involving the accidental death of a child.
22. Promotion of inexperienced/incompetent officer over you.
23. Internal affairs investigation against self.
24. Barricaded suspect.
25. Hostage situation resulting from domestic disturbance.

SOURCE: James D. Sewell, Police Stress, *FBI Law Enforcement Bulletin*, April 1981, p. 9.

In extreme cases, such as when an officer has lost a spouse, just gone through a divorce, worked a case involving a dead child, or been involved in a shooting incident, it is wise to expect that pressure will be great and to respond with concern and understanding.

Attendance Records

Consistent lateness, requests to be excused on short notice, or

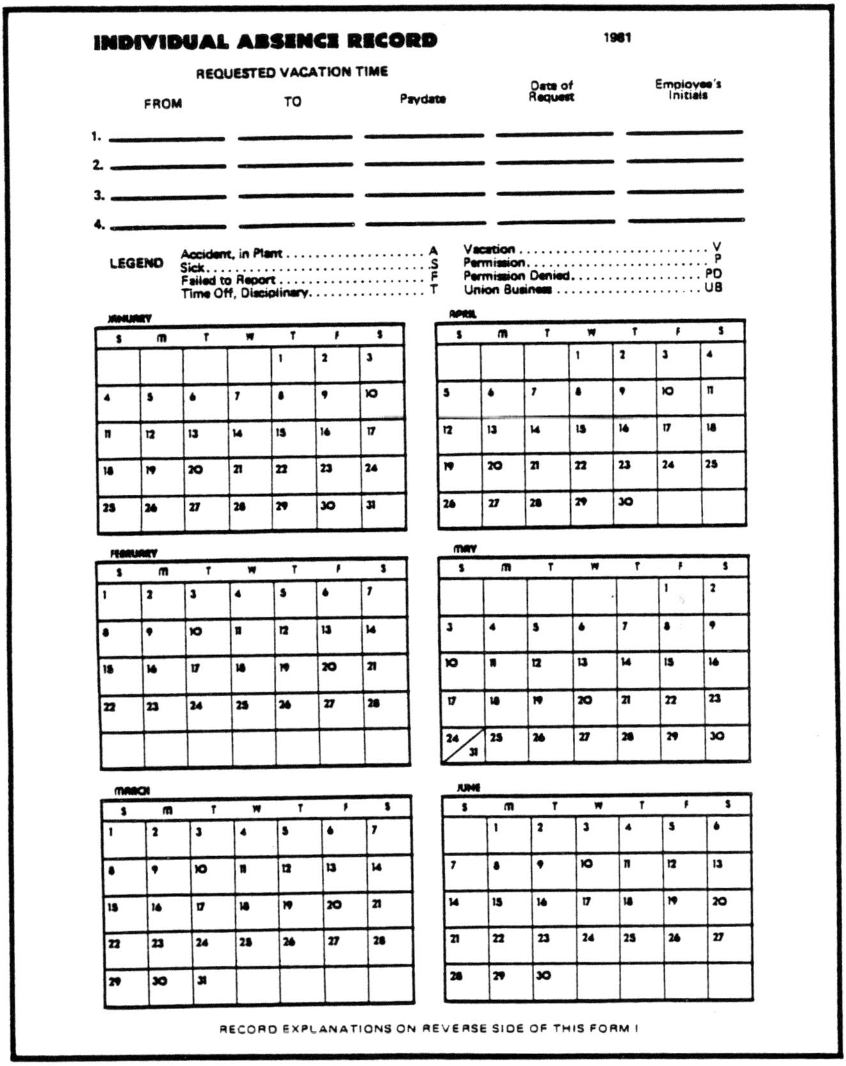

INDIVIDUAL ABSENCE RECORD 1981

REQUESTED VACATION TIME

	FROM	TO	Paydate	Date of Request	Employee's Initials
1.					
2.					
3.					
4.					

LEGEND
Accident, in Plant .... A
Sick .... S
Failed to Report .... F
Time Off, Disciplinary .... T
Vacation V
Permission .... P
Permission Denied .... PD
Union Business .... UB

JANUARY

S	M	T	W	T	F	S
				1	2	3
4	5	6	7	8	9	10
11	12	13	14	15	16	17
18	19	20	21	22	23	24
25	26	27	28	29	30	31

APRIL

S	M	T	W	T	F	S
			1	2	3	4
5	6	7	8	9	10	11
12	13	14	15	16	17	18
19	20	21	22	23	24	25
26	27	28	29	30		

FEBRUARY

S	M	T	W	T	F	S
1	2	3	4	5	6	7
8	9	10	11	12	13	14
15	16	17	18	19	20	21
22	23	24	25	26	27	28

MAY

S	M	T	W	T	F	S
					1	2
3	4	5	6	7	8	9
10	11	12	13	14	15	16
17	18	19	20	21	22	23
24/31	25	26	27	28	29	30

MARCH

S	M	T	W	T	F	S
1	2	3	4	5	6	7
8	9	10	11	12	13	14
15	16	17	18	19	20	21
22	23	24	25	26	27	28
29	30	31				

JUNE

S	M	T	W	T	F	S
	1	2	3	4	5	6
7	8	9	10	11	12	13
14	15	16	17	18	19	20
21	22	23	24	25	26	27
28	29	30				

RECORD EXPLANATIONS ON REVERSE SIDE OF THIS FORM !

Figure 3-1.

absences around vacation or days off may be a sign of problems. A tool for recognizing patterns in this behavior is a record that allows the supervisor to see an entire year at once. A form for this is presented in Figure 3-1.

Recognizing Stress Reactions in Oneself

There are two somewhat different kinds of stress reactions. One is the immediate reaction to pressure, the other is the result of too many demands for which one has inadequate resources. The first sort of reaction is an almost daily occurrence; a demand is placed on us, especially when we are frustrated or feel threatened and in danger (either physical or psychological). People have different symptoms in these situations: some feel a tightening in their chests, others experience a buzzing in their heads, still others feel their hearts racing. Usually in these situations we respond to the demand, and the feelings die down. Usually we can cope more or less effectively.

When stressors come too rapidly, however, or are too great and we lack the resources to deal with them, we may begin to experience more chronic and severe symptoms. Some of these are listed in Table 3-III. In going over this list, one must avoid self-diagnosis and, especially, self-medication. Physical symptoms, of course, should first be checked out with a physician. Also, presence of these symptoms should not be an excuse for excessive concern for one's health or for malingering. They are best taken as a signal of a need for reflection: to stop to take stock of one's life and one's goals and to search actively for ways to function more efficiently.

Table 3-III

STRESS SYMPTOMS

Below is a list of some of the conditions in which stress is thought to play a part. If any of these is experienced frequently or is severe, it may be a warning sign. One first step should be a thorough physical examination to rule out other causes.

Muscle aches (Especially of neck, shoulders, back, legs)
Extreme changes in appetite
Increased smoking or chain-smoking
Insomnia, nightmares
Increased sweating
Nausea, stomach pain, indigestion, ulcers
Grinding teeth

Headache, dizziness
Frequent low-grade infections
Rash or hives
Constipation or diarrhea
Loss of sex drive
High blood pressure, face flushing
Dry mouth or throat
Irritability or bad temper
Lethargy or inability to work
Cold, clammy, or clenched hands
Sudden bursts of energy, inability to relax
Depression or moodiness
Fear, panic, or anxiety
Fatigue, excessive sleepiness
Restlessness
Frequent colds, other respiratory infections
Rapid weight gain or loss
Allergic reactions, asthma attacks
Hyperventilation, shortness of breath
Increased number of minor accidents
Racing thoughts, inability to concentrate
Increased consumption of alcohol or tranquilizers
Feeling the need for a drink during or after work
Increased memory lapses
Changes in habitual behavior
Inability to enjoy work or play
Feelings of hopelessness, uselessness, despair
Thinking constantly about things you cannot change
Heart symptoms: acute anxiety attack
Tics, muscle twitches, muscle tension
Chronic illness for which doctor can find no specific cause

Finally, we should discuss "burnout" as a symptom of job malaise. The instrument used by Maslach to study this phenomenon is copyrighted, and is available from Consulting Psychologists Press, 577 College Avenue, Palo Alto, California 94306. Sample items (Maslach 1982, p. 8) include the following:

Emotional Exhaustion subscale
  Sample items:
    I feel emotionally drained from my work.
    Working with people all day is really a strain for me.
  Frequency patterns:
    High burnout — several times a month or more
    Low burnout — several times a year or less
Depersonalization subscale
  Sample items:
    I've become more callous toward people since I took this job.
    I worry that this job is hardening me emotionally.

Frequency patterns:
   High burnout — once a month or more
   Low burnout — once or twice a year, or less
Personal Accomplishment subscale (reverse scoring)
   Sample items:
   In my work, I deal with emotional problems very calmly.
   I feel I'm positively influencing other people's lives through my
work.
   Frequency patterns:
   High burnout — less than once a week
   Low burnout — several times a week or daily

NOTES

1. The psychologist, psychiatrist, or other professional interested in behavior change will, it is hoped, forgive the authors if they do not adhere strictly to the classification schemes of DSM III. The purpose here is to give rough guidelines, not to present a sophisticated treatise on psychiatric diagnosis.

2. The authors will discuss ways the administrator or supervisor might handle talk of suicide more fully in Chapter 4.

3. An acute anxiety attack is a stress-related problem that mimics a heart attack and may be related to spurts of adrenaline. Although the authors have no specific figures on the incidence of anxiety attacks in police compared with other occupations, it is their opinion that they are relatively common. For further information on the condition, see any good abnormal psychology text, such as Coleman, Butcher, and Carson (1980).

4. Hans Toch and his colleagues, in cooperation with the Oakland, California, police department, developed an exciting, innovative program for dealing with overly aggressive officers using peer counselors (Toch, Grant, and Galvin, 1975).

Chapter 4

ORGANIZATIONAL AND SUPERVISORY STRATEGIES FOR STRESS MANAGEMENT

Introduction

CHAPTERS 1 and 2 discussed the importance of organizational and supervisory styles in alleviating or exacerbating stress reactions. As was intimated there, the authors consider these levels critical: even the best, most dedicated individual will find it difficult to do the job and may develop stress reactions if he lacks appropriate support from the organization.

In addition to considerations of efficient functioning and humanitarian concerns about the welfare of workers, departments have another reason to be concerned about the quality of management and the reduction of stress. This reason is a legal one. Stress is being used increasingly — and with some success — to gain disability pensions. Administrators and supervisors also face the prospect of vicarious liability suits for failing to give proper support and training to their officers. Indeed, the powers of police administrators to discipline increasingly are being held up to legal scrutiny to determine what is proper and appropriate.

Change at this level, however, is the most complex and, sadly,

most likely to be resisted. This resistance may come from several
sources; first, of course, is from those at the top who see change as a
threat to their power. Resistance can, however, come from the bottom of the hierarchy. The more an organization is seen by the rank
and file members as unresponsive to their needs and concerns, the
more they are likely to resist change, even change that might benefit
them, seeing it as yet another of management's "scams." Too frequently, an oganization is in chaos — with stress reactions among
employees all too obvious — before it is motivated for change.[1] For
example, American auto manufacturers resisted changing to
management styles that have brought the Japanese success until
their backs were against the wall.

As with other public institutions, police departments are somewhat insulated by the lack of a clear "bottom line." Good policing often is difficult to define. As Toch (1971) has pointed out.

> police productivity as it is usually recorded is not reflective of quality
> policing. . . It may result in hoarded information, rushed services,
> and antagonized citizens. It may also bring a rush for "numbers" and a
> lowering of morale. Nonarresting officers may become second-class
> citizens, implictly nonproductive. For other officers, skilled work
> (such as prevention and peacekeeping) becomes "not police work," and
> is conducted "on the side." The well-rounded image of the organization
> becomes tarnished by its reward system and its accounting procedures
> (pp. 43 – 44).

Another problem deserves mention here. Often police administrators, and administrators of other institutions in the public sector, inveigh about political intervention in their operations. "If
only," they say, "the politicians would leave us alone and let us do
our job." The authors believe this view is naive. Police are, in the
final analysis, public servants, and politicians represent, however
inadequately, the will of that public. It is more realistic to accept
the inevitability of political influence and work through and with
it.

It is far beyond the scope of this book to cover innovations in
management technique in detail, and the authors would not wish to
patronize police administrators among the readers by too simplistic
a rendering of these theories; the majority of command level officers
are familiar with modern management theory. Therefore, concepts
that are in the vanguard of management theory will be presented,
and their importance for the development of the smoothly function-

ing organization, which is the best inoculation against stress, will be reiterated.

Although the authors continue to argue for more global proactive, preventive measures, in this chapter they will deal with specific programs aimed at crisis management and with problems of officers who are showing stress symptoms.

Stress and Organizational Style

Current management theory promotes the involvement of individuals at every level of the work hierarchy in making decisions about the jobs they do; participatory management is consistent with the primary needs of modern workers (Ouchi, 1981; Hampton, Summer, and Webber, 1978; Roberg, 1979). This theory is exemplified in the organizational structure called team policing (Gay et al., 1975; Sherman et al., 1973; Murphy and Block, 1970; Brown and Martin, 1976).

Although there is no direct evidence of the effectiveness of team policing in decreasing stress-related disorders, in some cases team policing has been generally successful both in fulfilling the police mandate and in improving morale (Ellison and Buckhout, 1981; Tortoriello and Blatt, 1974). Unfortunately, team policing gained the status of fad. In departments that wished to display "innovation without change" (Kaplan, 1975) — to appear to be modern without any change in basic power structures — team policing has meant stenciling "Neighborhood Police Team" on several radio cars or assigning several officers to attend more meetings of community groups (Ellison and Buckhout, 1981). It is hardly surprising that team policing was less than successful under these circumstances.

Another set of techniques of participatory management that is gaining currency in law enforcement are the mutual goal-setting techniques of management by objectives (Roberg, 1980; Kazoroski, 1980; Stewart, 1980). When goals are set at the policymaking level, departmental orders should be reviewed to assure that they are consistent with each other and with the goals. This practice would help relieve the role ambiguity that is seen by officers as a major source of pressure. The challenge here is to give guidance without removing discretion.

Progressive Discipline[2]

It has been a common practice in departments with which the authors are familiar to let inappropriate behavior continue until it became flagrant and then to discipline with suspensions or attempts at discharge.[3] Part of the rationale seems to have been to "give a person enough rope to hang himself." Frequently supervisors and administrators have failed to document this inappropriate behavior adequately and have relied on hearsay. In one case an officer had been late over eighty days in one year before any official notice was taken of this behavior. The department then attempted — unsuccessfully — to dismiss him.

In recent years officers have increasingly been going to court to protest such administrative actions. The courts often have upheld officers' claims that discipline was arbitrary and unreasonable. Management has been told that, in letting inappropriate behavior go unchallenged, it has failed to exercise management prerogative and thus has given up that right. Courts have further held that supervisors have a duty to train and counsel officers, working with them on ways to improve their performance. Progressive discipline is built on this concept.

Progressive discipline involves a series of increasingly severe sanctions.[4] At each stage the supervisor or administrator not only must inform the employee that his behavior is inappropriate but must also demonstrate that he has attempted to identify any problems leading to this behavior and provide counseling to resolve them. It is also crucial that all employees be disciplined in the same way for the same infractions.

The first step is an oral warning. For example, the officer is told formally by his supervisor that he has been late five days in the past month. He is asked if he is aware of the department's policy on lateness and is given a copy of that policy. The supervisor then attempts to identify the problem with him and works with him on solutions. A note on this interaction is made and kept in the officer's file.

If the behavior continues and the officer continues to report late for his tour at a rate that is above that which the department considers acceptable, the next step is a written warning, a copy of which is also kept on file. Again, the supervisor must work with the employee to correct the behavior.

Written warnings are followed by increasingly lengthy suspensions, of perhaps one day, then three days, then five days. At each step, documentation of attempts at helping the officer should be provided. If these steps are unsuccessful, it may then be appropriate for the department to begin administrative action for dismissal.

The Department Psychologist

The suggestion is frequently made that departments should employ mental health professionals to help officers deal with stressors (Reiser, 1972; Chandler, 1980; Stratton, 1980; Fenster and Schlossberg, 1979). Others have warned that any help that might come from interaction with a department psychologist or psychiatrist would be offset by the lack of confidentiality and, indeed, that therapy is seriously compromised because the therapist's first loyalty is to the department that pays him rather than to the officer-client. Thus, anything the officer tells the therapist can be included in his personnel record and used against him in departmental actions (Morris, 1980). Several writers have even suggested that company therapists be considered double agents, required to give Miranda warnings to clients (Szasz, 1967; Powledge, 1980).

Department psychologists (psychiatrists and other professionals concerned with behavior change) perform a number of functions: selection, training and evaluation, and counseling for officers showing the effects of chronic pressures. Often the same person is used for all of these tasks. The authors would like to suggest another alternative: that an organizational psychologist be used for the tasks of selection and training and evaluation rather than a clinician, who is typically called upon by departments. It is often possible to hire such people as consultants when they are needed, rather than to have them permanently on staff. Some departments have found that they can arrange collaborative efforts with a local university's psychology or business departments in which students do some of the work, under the supervision of professors. The quality of the work is not damaged, but the cost tends to be decreased substantially.

Recently, clinical psychologists have found another role in police departments. They have been called upon to work with officers who have just been involved in potentially traumatic incidents such as a shooting or working with horribly mutilated child victims. The city of Fremont, California, has a standard procedure stating that the department psychologist shall be involved "whenever an officer's actions on duty result in death or critical injury to another person, whether or not a shooting was involved" and may be called at the discretion of the officer's immediate supervisor "whenever an on-duty officer's life has been in critical danger (whether or not injury was sustained) or the officer has, in the performance of duty, witnessed an unusually traumatic injury or accident." Confidentiality is assured.[5]

The Washington State Patrol has a similar program, offering "post-critical incident" counseling for its officers. They, too, assure confidentiality. However, they have another advantage. Their psychologist, Dr. David H. Smith, was himself a trooper before he returned to school to complete a degree in clinical psychology; he is still a sworn officer. Because he is known to the men with whom he works as someone who has "been there," and because he was out of the "field" only a relatively short time, his credibility is increased.

Other departments have a referral list of outsiders who are called in to assist with posttraumatic counseling. It is always best if these professionals have a sound reputation among the officers and if confidentiality is assured by the officer's superior. Sometimes these referrals are handled by organizations such as the officer's union, the PBA or FOP; this increases the assurance of confidentiality.

Although the authors applaud attempts to work with officers who have handled assignments that have the potential to induce crisis, they have some reservations about calling in a psychological professional automatically and immediately. The authors believe the most important support in these situations comes from peers, a belief held by Symonds (1969). Referral to a psychologist runs the risk of setting up a self-fulfilling prophecy. The officer who might have been able to handle the situation is led to believe that there is something wrong with him if he is coping well and does not display a plethora of symptoms. An understanding that such referrals are routine, and an emphasis by the psychologist on the officer's strengths, can overcome this somewhat, if the psychologist is considered credible. It is crucial that the people who handle such situations be different from those who evaluate officers for potential dismissal on psychiatric grounds.

Another problem is the tendency to allege psychological damage to obtain a disability benefit. This may encourage officers to exaggerate trauma.

In some situations, of course, the department wants to use psychiatric testimony as support in dismissing an officer whose behavior is inappropriate, and who might prove dangerous. In these cases the wisest course is to refer the officer to the department surgeon and let him make the referral to a psychiatrist. This will save the person making the referral from a later charge that he had insufficient knowledge of psychological disorder and therefore was inappropriate in making a referral to a psychological professional. The supervising officer should, of course, inform the department surgeon in detail of the behavior that led to the referral. It is important to remember that in these cases, the professional is paid by the department and, as such, is its agent.

Special Programs: Prevention and Crisis Intervention

PHYSICAL FITNESS. Many departments have programs aimed at reducing the negative consequences of pressure through physical fitness. These range from providing a gym for officers to use on their own time to comprehensive services. The Union, New Jersey, police department provides a model of a comprehensive program.

> **Case 4:1.** Union, New Jersey, has a department
> of 133 sworn officers and approximately 19 civilian
> personnel. All police department employees and
> members of their families are eligible to participate
> in the program. Union is a suburban community of
> 50,000 in the greater New York area. The program
> is headed by a sworn officer who has a teaching cer-
> tificate in physical education. This is his full-time as-
> signment. Their facility, housed in a few basement
> rooms, includes a variety of equipment such as a
> treadmill, a Nautilis® machine, and a sauna. (This
> equipment was obtained through grants.) Officers
> who wish to participate must have permission from
> their physician; older officers are required to take a
> "stress test," which is largely paid for by the depart-
> ment. Officers are allowed to spend up to three
> hours a week of department time in the program.

Particularly important is that the chief and deputy chiefs support the program wholeheartedly and are enthusiastic participants. The program has been enthusiatically received and is to be expanded.

RETIREMENT PLANNING. The problems presented by the practice of encouraging early retirement and by the subjective reaction of feeling trapped by the pension were described earlier. Programs that help an officer plan for retirement decrease this stress. In fact, the military begins working with its career officers as early as ten years before the scheduled retirement date.

A number of programs of this sort are available. Unions or fraternal organizations might find this a useful service to offer to members, in addition to departmental program.

POSTTRAUMATIC INCIDENTS COUNSELING. It is important that departments have some procedure for helping officers deal with incidents that could be traumatic. This can involve training of supervisors to counsel such officers, peer counseling programs, or professional support. One such professional program was cited previously. Peer counselors must be carefully screened to weed out those who are using this as an opportunity to work out their own problems. One peer counseling program that reported great success was that of the Oakland police department, which worked with officers whose behavior was inappropritely aggressive (Toch, Grant, and Galvin, 1975). This format could be modified to fit other problems.

Special Programs: Chronic Problems

ALCOHOLISM. It is generally believed that alcoholism is rife among police officers. It goes without saying that alcohol abuse is a special problem among people who carry firearms. In some states, alcoholism is legally considered a disease, and a department must prove that it has attempted to rehabilitate an alcoholic officer before it attempts to dismiss him.

It is generally accepted that alcoholism is best dealt with by peers in groups such as Alcoholics Anonymous. Several departments have instituted special programs to deal with the alcoholic officer. Some, like those of the New York City police department, are department sponsored. Although the programs are well intentioned, they suffer the problems discussed earlier of counseling that can appear in an officer's file and later be used against him.

Another approach to alcoholism is a program set up and controlled by officers, perhaps with the sponsorhip of a police organization such as the PBA. One such program has been functioning for several years in New Jersey. In the beginning it was called the Law Enforcement Alcoholism Program (LEAP), but "alcoholism" has since been changed to "assistance" in the name in recognition of the wide variety of problems officers face.

> **Case 4:2.** LEAP was founded by Sgt. John Masterson, a recovered alcoholic who works with the East Orange, New Jersey, police department. Over 500 people have been helped during the first two years of operation. It is a volunteer organization, which is maintained by contributions and is working on a shoestring. It maintains a hot line to work with troubled officers and supports special Alcoholics Anonymous chapters for law enforcement personnel. Volunteers also are available to respond to the call "Come get me" and to facilitate entrance into detoxification programs. These volunteers will go to the officer's superiors to explain the treatment program and the officer's legal rights. Confidentiality is assured. LEAP volunteers will work with family members, co-workers, and superiors to give them help in dealing with the alcoholic.[5]

SUICIDE. Any talk of suicide should be taken very seriously. It is common for people who are thinking about taking their own lives to joke about it at first. Others often disregard this warning with dire consequences. It is not helpful in the long run if the individual succeeds in getting something he wants by threatening suicide; this simply teaches him to use the threat again in the future.

In threatened suicide cases the best course generally is referral to professional help, such as the department psychologist or police surgeon. The superior (or other person to whom the suicidal officer speaks) can say something such as the following: "I understand that things are bad for you, and I'm sorry you feel that life isn't worth living. Looking at it as an outsider, I would have thought that you had a lot to live for, but that's a decision only you can make. Before you do anything, I think you should speak to a professional about what's happening in your life, to see what your options really are."

Supervisory Strategies for Stress Management

Stress management, as noted in Chapters 1 and 2, has many implications for the first-line supervisor. First, he can be a key in causing or ameliorating stress in his subordinates. Second, the position of first-line supervisor is itself stressful. In a police department it is he who is the major link between rank and file officers and the department. If this is his first supervisory position, he is often in an ambivalent role: still close to his former peers, yet part of management. Many sergeants have told us that when they were first promoted and attempted to discipline their subordinates, their efforts were greeted with comments of, "Who do you think you are? Why, only a few weeks ago you were one of us; you've done the same things yourself!"

Management, too, often is not clear about the role it wants sergeants to take. They are neither fish nor fowl in management's eyes; they are expected to control and discipline the troops and are given no input into departmental decisions. Some sergeants also perform supervisory tasks, while for others the promotion is just a way to grant a pay raise with few changes in status or duties. This, truly, is the role ambiguity that has been found to be so stressful. Because the effects of stress at the higher levels radiate downward, their subordinates also feel these pressures.

Cognitive variables also play a role in self-image and behavior of supervisors. Some supervisors feel threatened by particularly competent subordinates and seem almost to go out of their way to denigrate a competent person's strengths, to expose his weaknesses, or to make his job more difficult. Another way of viewing a subordinate who excels is as a compliment to one's own leadership and abilities as a trainer. Such a person reflects well on his supervisor. It is the responsibility of every supervisor to train subordinates to take his place. The supervisor who takes such a stance tends to increase efficiency and decrease the pressure on himself.

The first-line supervisor has an advantage; if he has had any training in supervision, he already knows the basics of stress management.[7] Good supervision itself is the best stress-management tool. Good supervisory techniques not only increase efficiency but also help officers withstand outside pressures. In contrast, inappropriate supervision can itself be one of the worst sources of pressure. Trojanowicz (1980) puts it as follows:

> Any sound organization with well-trained personnel can withstand heavy pressures from outside without cracking, but when the stress comes from inside, its members are much more vulnerable. This is particularly true in the police culture, where, lacking positive feedback from the public, officers must turn to their peers for necessary social support. If they are accused and feel rejection by people within their own ranks, the effect can be devastatingly stressful, because they may feel both a sense of betrayal and a sense of desperation, that they have nowhere else to turn (p. 236).

It is beyond the scope of this book to review the principles of supervision extensively.[8] However, a quick reminder of some that touch particularly on stress management seems in order. As has been previously discussed, role conflict and role ambiguity are important sources of stress from the organization. The worker does not know what is expected of him, or he receives conflicting demands. He is usually helped by clear directions about the tasks to be done: both what to do and how to do them (Aldang and Brief, 1978). He must be kept informed of his progress. The supervisor who sets goals clearly for his people, who lets them know exactly what will win approval and what will result in punishment, is relieving this sort of tension.

There is, however, a contradiction here. Structure decreases role ambiguity, but it can also lead to rigidity, stifling creativity and the exercise of discretion (Toch, 1978). Achievement of a balance is no small challenge for the police supervisor or administrator.

The mention of reward and punishment leads to the topic of motivation: what, precisely, do people find rewarding, and under what conditions is punishment most effective? Particularly, what sorts of rewards and punishments are within the control of a first-line supervisor? Because individuals differ in motivation, answers to this question are complex. However, a few general statements may be made.

Research has consistently demonstrated that reward works best to gain desired behaviors. While punishment may be effective in extinguishing undesirable activities, it does not lead to improved behavior. Unfortunately, too many supervisors ignore good behavior, believing that praise is inappropriate when someone is "just doing his job." Worse, they punish inconsistently. Much of the time they ignore infractions of the rules and only punish when someone else notices and it reflects directly on them. Other supervisors take offense at some violations while winking at others.[9]

Punishment, if it is to work, should be swift, certain, and appropriate to the violation. Not only should the offender know exactly why he is being punished, but he also needs to know what behavior will result in reward in the future and, perhaps, to be trained in that behavior. The cycle of ignoring good behavior and capricious punishing may lead to "learned helplessness" (see Chapter 1) or to the "low profile," which borders on malingering.

A potent form of reward and punishment available to first-line supervisors is praise or reprimand. Norfolk (1980, pp. 94-95) has discussed the conditions under which each works best. His findings follow.

Effects of Praise and Reprimand on Quality and Quantity of Work
(In order of success)
1. Public praise (87.5 success rate)
2. Private reprimand
3. Public reprimand
4. Private ridicule
5. Public ridicule
6. Private sarcasm
7. Public sarcasm (deterioration of performance in 65.1% of cases)

Progressive Discipline for Supervisors

The first-line supervisor has primary responsibility for the first steps in the chain of progressive discipline that was discussed earlier in this chapter, the oral and written warnings. Usually it is he who first becomes aware of violations or inappropriate behavior. Many supervisors hesitate to discipline formally. They let a behavior, such as chronic tardiness or even evidence of drinking on duty go unpunished, or they fail to document it properly. When the extent of the violation becomes flagrant, so discipline can no longer be avoided, there is no evidence to back up the charges. In this era of frequent litigation, especially given the rise in vicarious liability suits, attention to the documentation that progressive discipline requires protects the supervisor.

Progressive discipline should also offer aid to the supervisor who is uncomfortable disciplining subordinates. Its first aim, as described earlier, is to identify inappropriate behavior early and, through counseling, to rehabilitate the offender and protect his job.

Interviewing and Counseling

Police supervisors often feel uncomfortable interviewing and counseling subordinates. Part of this is the discomfort that comes from having to tell someone else he is not performing up to standard, but part is from a hesitancy to pry and a fear that the subordinate will begin to ventilate feelings, which the supervisor feels inadequate to handle. Supervisors will sometimes object to discussions of this in texts and training courses. They argue vociferously that it is not a supervisor's task to be his brother's keeper. The authors disagree, as does every text in police supervision they have ever read. This is a vital tool in the supervisor's larger concern for efficiency and morale.

Interviews and counseling are appropriate not only when a problem develops but on a routine basis, at least once every three months. These routine interviews should be performance reviews, examining progress, especially commending satisfactory work, and setting new goals and objectives. These goals and objectives must be realistic.[10] Earlier chapters of this book discussed at length the importance of prediction and understanding in reducing stress and said that it is preferable to know what to expect, even if it is unpleasant, than to have it come by surprise. It is no favor to delude a person, allowing him to think that his work is satisfactory or that he has potential for promotion when in fact, to the best of the supervisor's knowledge, this is not so.

Interviews between subordinates and supervisors often are stressful for both parties. The routine interview helps alleviate this somewhat. When subordinates become accustomed to the idea of routine interviews, they realize that to be called into the supervisor's office is not always a signal for alarm, that one is in trouble. They find that interviews can be occasions for praise, as well as criticism.

Situations that call for interview and counseling are of two kinds: a check on suspicions that chronic problems exist and support in an acute crisis.

Basic interviewing techniques appropriate for use in the routine interview are covered fully in texts on police supervision, such as those listed earlier. They also discuss counseling for problem employees, those showing the signs of chronic pressure. This section will, therefore, review the tactics for dealing with problem employees only briefly.

First, it is best that the supervisor who observes behavior changes of the sort described previously (in Chapter 3) investigate them as soon as possible, not wait, hoping they will go away. This is particularly so if the behavior involves performance of official duties. The interview's introductory comments can then focus on these problems. The supervisor can approach the problem with comments such as, "I'm concerned about you; your work recently hasn't been what it should be (or, has not been up to your usual standards), and I want to see what I can help you do about it." The specific problems should then be detailed, and very specific procedures for their amelioration set forth.

The appropriate atmosphere for an interview of this kind is one that encourages discovering the problem and working together to find solutions for it. The interviewer should avoid making remarks about the subordinate's character — "You're nothing but a goof-off." — or his intentions — "Are you trying to make me look bad or something?" Arguing and fault finding tend to make subordinates respond defensively and are seldom productive.

In this, as in other interviews, body language is important. The "official reprimand" interview is one where the subordinate stands in front of the superior's desk. A problem-solving, counseling approach is better achieved if the two sit with no barrier between them. Eye contact and voice tone also help set an appropriate atmosphere.

Even when the supervisor's emphasis is on performance, at times the subordinate will excuse his actions with descriptions of his personal problems. This calls for firmness and tact from the supervisor, as well as an open mind. The subordinate may, indeed, have serious personal problems that are beyond his control.

One approach is to express understanding but to continue to emphasize the importance of job performance. It may be appropriate to work with the officer briefly on possible solutions to these personal problems and, if they seem severe, to suggest sources for professional help: investment or credit counseling for money problems, marriage counseling, and the like.

Sometimes employees come on their own to ask for help and advice. The supervisor first needs to determine the willingness to change. Does this person really want help, or is this an elaborate overture to an excuse? Even those who want help may not be able to discuss all the details of a problem at once. It may take time for the officer to test the supervisor's trustworthiness. The employee should be allowed to proceed at his own pace, even if it takes several interviews. There is, of course, a limit to this; the supervisor's time is valuable, too, and he should see definite progress. Otherwise, he may find that he is encouraging a chronic complainer.

When the employee is sincere, the supervisor may find that simply listening is sufficient, that as the employee talks he will find his own solutions. If this does not work, a referral may be in order. Specificially, the supervisor should avoid the temptation to play amateur analyst and give advice. This is particularly true for family problems.

In contrast to the employee who talks willingly about problems, others react to any suggestion that something might be wrong with vehement denial: "I'm all right! There's nothing wrong with me! Mind your own business." In this case, if the supervisor was checking out a hunch, for example, that the officer had been looking tired lately (although his performance did not seem to be affected), it often is appropriate to accept his version at the time. The supervisor might say, "Okay, I can certainly admit to being wrong in a case like this, but I like to check these things out. I'm glad to hear that everything's okay; if you do find that there is anything bothering you and think I might be able to help, let me know and we'll see what we can do to try to help you straighten it out." This may provide an opening so that several days later the officer may come back and say that, yes, something is wrong. Alternatively, this observation may alert the officer, telling him that others have noticed changes in his behavior and lead him to seek other sources of help.

Special problems that are common in police include alcoholism and trouble in the home, including financial difficulties. While the symptoms of problem drinking tend to be easy to spot, there is a tendency to deny that a person has a problem until it is fairly far advanced. Drinking is often part of the expectation of the police subculture, and officers brag of drunken escapades. They frequently get together in a bar at the end of a shift to wind down and exchange war stories; it is an acceptable way to ventilate.[11]

Chronic lateness, calls requesting a day off at the last minute for personal reasons, extended weekends, and obvious hangovers are but a few of the symptoms of alcoholism. However, if asked about it, the problem drinker will deny that he is having trouble controlling his drinking and become defensive about it. Family members may be the ones who first ask for help.

The supervisor should not attempt to counsel the alcoholic on his own but should refer him to the police surgeon or recommend an organization such as Alcoholics Anonymous. Indeed, some localities have AA chapters made up entirely of police officers. If the man refuses to go, the supervisor will then need to begin disciplinary action.

Family problems sometimes surface when a spouse calls the station asking for help. It is usually best for the supervisor not to become directly involved in marital disputes, and it is especially unwise to take sides. One way to deal with this situation is to say something such as "What you folks need is a referee," and make a referral. If the dispute involves assault, the problem becomes much more serious and should be handled the same as any serious complaint against an officer.

Counseling for Acute Crisis

Techniques for working with subordinates in acute crisis, especially that brought on by accidental stressors, has received less attention in the supervision tests than have counseling for chronic problems. The support of his supervisor can be of great help to a man who has been involved in a shooting, been injured, worked with child victims, been present at the scene of a disaster, or been subjected to other stressors described in Chapter 2. New officers may need special support in their first experiences with accidents, mutilated bodies, and the like.

In these settings, time is important.[12] It is in the acute crisis phase that the person is most vulnerable and suggestible and that intervention is most effective. The supervisor can express his concern and acknowledge that this is a difficult time. He can also remind the subordinate that it is appropriate to be upset or feel bad at times such as those and that it probably will take some time to recover. The supervisor can go over with him the crisis reactions described in Chapter 1 so that he understands that these reactions are normal and not a sign that he is a poor officer or less of a man. Women officers generally are somewhat more comfortable expressing feelings of this sort and are less likely to see them as a reflection on their capabilities; however, they, too, need support at these times.

People who are in acute crisis need much more active intervention than do those struggling with chronic problems. It may be appropriate for the person intervening to give specific directions or to do much more talking and explaining than would be appropriate with chronic problems. If the person seems to want to discuss his problems, this should be allowed, but no attempt should be made to force it. Also, when ventilation deteriorates into self-pity, it should be steered back to "What can you learn from this?" and "What can you do to make it better in the future?"

It is not always appropriate for the sergeant or lieutenant to be the one to provide support, especially for a young officer or in departments in which the rank structure is very rigid. He may find it best to ask an experienced officer of the same rank to talk with the man who may be in crisis.

Most officers who have been involved in a shooting find it particularly helpful to talk with someone who has had a similar experience. In these cases, the sergeant or lieutenant can express his concern but then suggest that many people in that situation benefit from talking to someone who has "been there" and offer to make the contact.

If possible, it is usually best for the officer who has been in crisis to stay on the job or to take only a short time off, and supervisors can encourage this.

> **Case 4:3.** An officer told us of an experience that he felt played a part in his ability to work effectively on accident scenes. With only eight days on the job, he found himself the first at the scene of a particularly grisly accident. When the sergeant pulled up, five minutes later, he found the officer in a shouting

match with a bystander. No flares had been placed
and traffic was backing up. The sergeant walked
quickly over and said, "I'll take over here. You get
the flares out and get started getting that traffic
moving." Afterwards, he sat with the officer for a few
minutes over a cup of coffee in a diner. "Man, that
one bothered me. You never really get used to them.
Sometimes I'll go by the scene afterwards, and it will
all flash back to me. It helps me to take a deep breath
and just think about what I have to do and not about
those bodies. It's tough to stay professional, but it
just makes things worse when you take your feelings
out on people at the scene." The officer felt that this
restored his dignity and gave him some coping strategies, which he has used frequently in his career.

Summary

The overall effectiveness of any department depends on the quality of its management and its supervisors. Good personnel without
leadership can do only so much. Inappropriate supervision and
management that shows no concern for their needs are among the
chief items that officers list as stressful. Good management is a complex task of balancing the needs of the organization against the needs
of the subordinates, in itself a stressful situation. The rewards of performing well, however, are great. While the manager or supervisor
cannot save or rehabilitate all his problems, he can go far toward
buffering his department or squad against the stressors of the job,
creating a cohesive unit with high morale.

NOTES

1. When a department is in very bad shape, it may be nearly impossible for current administrators to turn it around. In these cases,
outside consultants may be needed. A case history of one department's success with organizational development is found in Boss
(1979).

2. The authors wish to thank attorney Thomas Savage for intro-
ducing them to these concepts. In addition to providing legal protec-

tion, they are consistent with good management practice. The authors would caution, however, that they be used only as guidelines and that each department check with its attorney on local rulings.

3. Often, it has been noted, hidden personal or political agendas are involved in disciplinary actions of this sort.

4. For severe infractions, such as larceny, the first steps would, of course, be skipped.

5. The authors are indebted to Robert Wasserman, Chief of Police of the City of Fremont, California, for permission to use these excerpts. More complete information about this policy, Operations Directive Log: 77-2, Date: 2/18/77, Index: p-7 may be obtained from him.

6. Captain Neal Coleman of the East Orange police department, one of the volunteers in this program, supplied this information.

7. The authors have been shocked at the number of police supervisors who have received no formal training for their role.

8. Some supervisory texts the authors have found helpful are Roberg (1979), Trojanowicz (1980), and Iannone (1980).

9. Obviously it would be impossible for any supervisor to enforce all rules rigidly, just as it is impossible for any officer to enforce all laws to the letter. The authors are not suggesting that discretion is inappropriate. It is, rather, the capricious and arbitrary imposition of discipline that is harmful.

10. The authors find Steward (1980) a very helpful reference for specifics of goal setting for investigators.

11. Richard Clement, former chief of police in Dover Township, New Jersey, and former president of the International Association of Chiefs of Police, had, for many years, a unique program in which officers were allowed to drink beer together in the station house at the end of a shift. The tendency to drink and its help in ventilation were, thus, carefully controlled.

12. Here again the authors draw on the work of Martin Symonds, head of the New York City police department's Psychological Services Unit and on interviews with David Smith, psychologist for the Washington state police.

Chapter 5

TECHNIQUES FOR INDIVIDUAL STRESS
MANAGEMENT I

Introduction

BECAUSE the net of stress has been cast so broadly, many kinds
of preventive techniques have been caught up in it. This chapter and the next will consider some of the strategies that have been
offered to individuals who are feeling the symptoms of stress. Research support for each will be presented, with special emphasis on
research with police. The techniques themselves will be described —
at least briefly — specific exercises for those readers who wish to try
some of them will be given, and reference sources for those who wish
to explore further will be suggested. As before, it must be emphasized that no one of these is the perfect strategy for everyone, but
most are, if not specifically useful for stress reduction, relatively
benign.

A major problem in all stress reduction programs is motivation.
Change in personal habits and ways of thinking is not easy. It involves admitting that there may be a problem and taking responsibility for doing something about it. This may mean giving up the
protection that cynicism and negativism afford. It may involve hard
choices; in this, as in other areas of life, there is no such thing as a

free lunch. Our goals often are mutually exclusive; thus, we must give up some of the things we would have liked for those that are more important.

Because change is difficult, a common strategy is to wait for a dramatic sign of trouble — such as a heart attack — before taking corrective measures. Another approach when symptoms of stress appear is to head for the medicine cabinet; it is easier to take a pill — or a drink — for temporary symptom relief than to confront and deal with problems. While in some cases denial may be the best strategy (Lazarus, 1979), and an occasional aspirin, or even drink, can get one over a rough spot, in general a steady routine of self-medication is unnecessary and potentially dangerous.

The authors prefer preventive strategies. They believe that, to be happy, people must assume responsibility for their own lives. The evaluation of how great the stressors are, how bad life is, how great the cost of change, and what strategies to use must rest with the individual. In severe cases, professional help may be in order, but even a professional cannot save a client or make decisions for him but can only help make options clearer.

Although overuse has brought it to the border of cliché, the maxim for personal stress management is expressed simply in the prayer of St. Francis, used by Alcoholics Anonymous, which asks for the serenity to accept what one cannot change, the courage to change what one can, and the wisdom to know the difference.

Goal Setting

Many of the strategies for stress management have as a starting point an assessment of goals and priorities. For those readers who wish to try this, Exercise 5:1 is presented.

Exercise 5:1. Goal setting.
Begin by making up a sheet similar to the one in Figure 5-1. Take ten minutes or so and list at least four goals in each category: lifetime goals, one-year goals, and one-month goals. Feel free to let your fancy have some rein and include personal and professional goals, but be as specific as possible. Try to limit yourselves to things you can measure so that you'll know when you have reached your goal. For example, list "make lieutenant" or "spend more time with my family" or "feel more relaxed much of the time" or "find better ways

to interact with my boss so that I don't walk out of his office in a rage half of the time" rather than "be happy." Also, limit your goals to things you can accomplish for yourself rather than things that are primarily the responsibility of others; for example, don't include goals such as "get my children married off."[1] Next, set priorities: mark each item "A" for very important, "B" for moderately important, or "C" for low priority.

GOALS

Personal	Priority	Professional	Priority

Lifetime Goals

One-Year Goals

One-Month Goals

Figure 5-1.

Now, check your list for inconsistencies. For example, it is very difficult to advance in a job and never take work home or to have six children and a great deal of personal freedom. Decide what is most important and modify or drop the conflicting goal. Then, break the very important items into manageable steps (especially those on the lifetime or one-year list). For example, a goal of "learn to play tennis" might involve as a first step checking with friends to find a teacher. Put these items on specific "To Do" lists (see Figure 5-2).

Having determined what is important, one now may look to ways to achieve these goals. As noted in Chapter 1, coping strategies are generally classified as focused toward problems or emotions. Coyne, Aldwin, and Lazarus (1981) point out that emotion-focused strategies (including changes in thoughts and feelings) are most appropriate when the individual is powerless to change the environment, and problem solving is best when change is possible. Consideration of stress management techniques in this chapter will begin with problem-focused strategies.

First, however, the authors must add a note on gimmickry. Some of the strategies presented could be called gimmicks, a term often used pejoratively. Jeremiads against "quick fix" solutions to problems in living continue to be popular with helping professionals and the public. As a culture we have bought the psychoanalytic idea that all problems, all distress, all inefficiency have roots in the residue of childhood traumas, that behavior change which does not come in the process of tortuous excavation of these roots is temporary at best, a calm before a storm of retribution from the unconscious. While in some cases this may be so, the evidence is less compelling than that which says that many problems come from lack of skills. A third-grade child who has low self-concept because he cannot read would do better with work at reading than with therapy for his self-image. In the same vein, Stotland (1975) describes the malignant effect of bad police management on the self-esteem of the average officer.

There is also evidence that people can and do change habits of long standing by themselves, without professional help — even habits that professionals have considered as intransigent as smoking, drug addiction, and overeating (Schachter, 1982). Many professionals who are in the business of behavior change are now giving their clients specific behavioral assignments (Garfield and Bergin,

1978; Foreyt and Rathjen, 1978).

Certainly, gimmicks are not the whole solution to long-standing, complex problems. In some cases, however, they provide a starting point and give one a sense of success, which may encourage a try at more difficult changes. In other cases, where the problem is a lack of simply-learned skills, gimmicks can go a long way toward relieving pressure.

Two commonsense solutions to stress look at the reports that say lack of time and lack of money loom large as problems for many people and suggest techniques for managing both.

Time Management

Many of us, it is said, find that we do not have enough time for everything we want to do. Often we discover that, although we have felt harried from the press of things demanding our attention and have worked long hours, we have spent our time doing relatively unimportant, time-consuming tasks while important ones have been neglected (Lakein, 1974).[2] Particularly, we are prone to spend time on unimportant tasks that seem pressing — especially if someone else is nagging us about them — while neglecting important tasks, ones that are consistent with long-range goals, for which there is little pressure. For example, it is easier for a person to give in to a spouse's request for help in rearranging the dining room than to start to write a paper that is part of that person's goal of advancing his career. Problems in managing time are especially common in people who exhibit the type A behavior pattern (Friedman and Rosenman, 1974), those who tend to take on too much and to feel especially pressed to achieve and accomplish many things. The specialization called time management offers relief from problems of this sort.[3]

Time management has become a fad among managers; articles on technique are common in management journals, and time management software is even available for the personal computer. Rational time management is said to help control the panicky feeling of too much to do with too little time to do it. It is sometimes used by therapists to give clients strategies for facing and clarifying decisions (Davis, Eshelman, and McKay, 1980). However, there is no research evidence to tell us whether or not time management schemes are effective in this goal of reducing feelings of stress or panic. We do not, for example, know how many people begin such a program full of enthusiasm only to let it drop within a few weeks or months.

Symptoms of poor time management include rushing, chronic vacillation between unpleasant alternatives, fatigue, or listlessness, with many slack hours of nonproductive activity, constantly missed deadlines, insufficient time for rest or personal relationships, a sense of being overwhelmed by demands and details and of having to do things that give little pleasure most of the time (Davis, Eshelman, and McKay, 1980).

Time management strategies seem particularly important for people who work at supervisory or executive jobs and who have some control over their work schedules. Much the same sorts of skills also are now being used by police managers to help set departmental priorities (Roberg, 1979), but the officer in a radio car, who is largely at the mercy of dispatcher and sergeant, may have to reserve time management for his personal life.

Some basic rules for time management (taken largely from Lakein [1974]), are the following:

1. The goal of time management is to achieve a balance in the scheduling of time — neither too rigid, i.e. compulsive, restrained, and restricting, nor too loose. One must guard against too rigid a schedule: build in time for interruptions, emergencies, and the like. Add a little time for the inevitable snafus. One must especially provide time for a personal life.

2. A basic premise of time management is that one cannot do everything there is to do, nor even everything one should do. One must make choices based on one's unique value system.

3. There is no single solution for time management that will work best for everyone.

4. Control of time starts with planning. If one plans each day, there will always be time for the important things. While people are sometimes controlled by unpredictable events, they also have a great deal of freedom in how to spend time.

5. Setting goals and establishing deadlines help avoid the negative consequences of Parkinson's law: "Work expands to fill the time available for its completion."

6. Get "absolute musts" out of the way early in the day when most people have more energy and can thus avoid feeling frantic

throughout the day.

7. Ask, "How terrible would it be if I didn't do this low priority item?" If the answer is "Not too terrible," do not do it. Items of small importance should be put aside unless one has finished all the more important tasks.

8. Procrastination can be attacked by —

a. setting up leading tasks (a physical step that leads you into a big job that you have been postponing);

b. making a commitment to someone else who is willing to offer support;

c. giving rewards for the completion of the project or tasks that will lead to the completion of the project;

d. recognizing that habits change slowly and starting small and selectively;

e. concentrating on one thing at a time.

9. Use periods of rest and diversion during the day to restore energy. It is inefficient to work when tired. A few minutes of rest, a stretch, or a walk around the office may improve productivity.

10. Handle each piece of paper only once.

11. Learn to say no. Unless it is a superior who asks, keep away from commitments that require large amounts of time to be spent on low priority items. Learn to say, "I don't have the time."

12. Set aside several periods a day to think and plan.

13. Cut off nonproductive activities as soon as possible.

14. Stop trying to be perfect; learn what the acceptable standard of efficiency is and work to that. Everyone makes mistakes. This does not mean, however, that one should condone shoddiness but that standards should be realistic.

Some people begin a time management program with a time log. This is a record of activities and the time they take over the course of a week or two. This device often helps in motivation because it demonstrates graphically the time spent on unimportant tasks. To keep a time log, one simply records on a sheet of paper all the activities of the day while going along, including the time each activity takes. Entries in a time log might look like this:

AM		*Time* (minutes)
6:00	Alarm goes off, lie in bed	20

6:20	Get up, take long shower	30
6:50	Shave, etc.	10
7:00	Breakfast	25
7:25	Dress	15
7:40	Leave for work; commute	30
8:10	Arrive at work 10 minutes late	

In analyzing a time log, one should ask the following questions about each task (as an example, the somewhat trivial task of lawn maintenance will be used):

1. *Do the results justify the amount of time?* Is it so important to have a perfect lawn that you spend an hour a day on it and have no time left for your family? What would the lawn look like if you only spent an average of three hours a week on it? *What evidence do you have that your expectations are accurate?* Does lawn maintenance mean more to you than external appearances, i.e. is it a form of relaxation?

2. *Is the task consistent with objectives or major goals?* Is "A home that the neighbors will envy" one of your most important goals?

3. *What is the relative importance of each task compared to others?* Is the envy of neighbors more important than time spent with family?

4. *Could the task be delegated? Under what conditions is delegation possible?* Is there a child in the neighborhood who cuts lawns? How good is his work? Can we afford it? *What evidence of this do you have?*

5. *Is the task really necessary?* Could you get just as much pleasure from a low maintenance landscaping scheme?

6. *When others are involved in performing the task, does this make good use of their time?* Is your spouse a klutz who ruins lawnmowers at a glance and has twice been cut by the hedge clipper, resulting in trips to the emergency room? Is the same spouse superb as a trader in antiques, able to spot bargains miles away and haggle like a professional? Is it worthwhile to have this spouse helping with the lawn chores, or would you be better off with the aforementioned child?

7. *When delays are encountered, what alternatives can be ready to work on?* On the job, low priority, easily accessible tasks can be used, e.g. when going to a meeting, one can take along something else in case a delay occurs.[+] (In the lawn example, if the landscaper fails to show up with the fill, it may be possible to spend time weeding, reading a book, preparing for the captain's exam, or bathing the dog.)

Assume the person whose time log was presented previously is unhappy because he is chronically late to work, which is getting him in trouble. He also wishes he had time to read the paper in the morning. An analysis of the two hours of his time log would indicate a possible savings of perhaps three-quarters of an hour if he gets up when the alarm rings and/or cuts shower and breakfast time. If his commuting route is a bad one, with frequent delays, extra time should be built into the schedule. If there are no delays on a particular day, that time could be spent at work reading the paper. The alarm also could be set later to allow more sleep, especially if this person lies in bed saying to himself, "I really should get up." Of course, some people feel they need such time to get going, and this may be an important item for them. They must set their own priorities. Certainly, the ten minutes of lateness experienced in the example could easily be avoided. The time log might then look something like this:

AM		*Time* (minutes)
6:30	Alarm goes off, get up	5
6:35	Take shower	10
6:45	Shave, etc.	10
6:55	Breakfast	10
7:05	Dress	15
7:20	Leave for work, commute	30
7:50	Arrive at work, read paper	10
8:00	Roll call	

Exercise 5:2. "To Do" list.

Another time management tool is the "To Do" list, an example of which is found in Figure 5-2.

Rules for the use of the "To Do" List are as follows:

1. Before beginning, think about how you work best. Do you find that your best thinking is the first thing in the morning, or are you a zombie until noon? Schedule tasks accordingly, with routine ones that require little thought at your low times.

2. Make a list of this sort for each day. It is usually best to keep several weeks' worth made up so that you can enter items as they come up.

3. List the items that require some action from you, and in the priority column rate each A, B, or C. Plan to do these items in order of their importance.

4. Among items of equal importance, take on first those which need to be done soonest. Evaluate the time you have available and create blocks of time for longer tasks. Keep a list of short tasks that you can do any time you are waiting or are "between things."

5. Put the items down on a daily calender; avoid being too compulsive; leave some time for interruptions and emergencies. Then *do* them. When you are finished with each major task, reward yourself with a cup of coffee, a walk down the hall, a short chat with a friend, or the like. Build these rewards into the schedule, but do not overdo it.

6. Cross out items as you complete them, and note your results.

7. Try to make phone calls in blocks, rather than scattering them throughout the day. Before the call, jot down the items you want to cover and cross them off as you go.

8. Jot down items needing work in the future under "long range," and once a week transfer them to a tickler file, or enter them on a planning sheet already made up for that day.

9. Before you leave work each day, transfer items you did not complete that were in the "important" category to a new planning sheet for the next day. Reevaluate low priority items to see if they may be eliminated before carrying them over. Ask yourself, "What is the thing most likely to happen if I don't get this done? What is the worst thing that could happen? How likely is that?"

10. On Fridays, take fifteen to twenty minutes to go over the week's items. Check to see if the items you labeled as very important are consistent with your goals. If you find many items of this sort, you may wish to rethink your stated goals. Then set up tasks for the next week. If, over the course of several weeks, you find that you frequently carry items over from day to day and week to week, you are probably overscheduling. Rethink your priorities and drop the unimportant items.

11. Realize that you will never get through the list, never be without something to do, and do not berate yourself for those things which are left undone. Instead, give yourself a pat on the back for what you have accomplished.

TO DO TODAY

NAME _____   DATE _____

PRIORITY	TASKS	DEADLINE	ESTIMATED TIME	RESULTS & ACTUAL TIME USED	PHONE CALLS (Name,Purpose)
					LETTERS, REPORTS TO WRITE

PEOPLE TO SEE./ DISCUSSION TOPICS

LONG RANGE (Task, When Due)

Figure 5-2.

Financial Planning

Many of the officers the authors interviewed about stress complained about money or financial problems as a major source of pressure. Although many people worry and complain about money, few are willing to take the time, effort, and responsibility to do anything rational about it: only about one-fourth of the people who report concern about money have any systematic plan for assessing their spending or have made a budget. Along the same lines, officers often feel compelled to take second and third jobs and seldom sit down first (with the family if they have one) and systematically assess spending to see if the material things these jobs would purchase are worth the time spent away from the family.[5]

A simple guide to assess the need for a budget follows.

Do You Need A Budget?

Answer *Yes* or *No* to each of the following questions.

_____ 1. Does your family fight about money frequently?

_____ 2. Do you find yourself using credit cards for all your purchases?

_____ 3. Do you find yourself falling behind in payments?

_____ 4. Do you find yourself juggling payments, especially for the essentials: paying the gas bill this month while letting the mortgage payment slide?

_____ 5. Have you considered (or actually taken out) a consolidation loan so that you will only have one large payment to make?

_____ 6. Have you or another member of the family taken, or considered taking, a second job just to pay current bills?

_____ 7. Are you borrowing for essentials: house payment, food, utilities, etc.?

_____ 8. Do you get dunning letters from creditors; has there ever been a threat to garnishee your wages?

_____ 9. Are you less than SURE where the money will come from to pay outstanding debts?

_____ 10. Is your checking account almost always in the red; do you frequently need to go to other sources, such as your "ready credit" from the bank or funds earmarked for other uses, such as children's college, to pay current expenses?

IF YOU ANSWER YES TO ANY OF THESE, YOU MAY WISH TO CONSIDER MAKING A BUDGET.

For those encouraged by the preceding guide to seek help, there are several sources. Many cities have a consumer credit counseling service, a nonprofit agency that gives confidential advice on budgets, credit, and debt management for very low fees — often free.[6] Many self-help books also are available. One the authors particularly like is *The H & R Block Family Financial Planning Workbook* by Susan Kelliher Ungaro (New York, Collier, 1980).

A final problem with money management comes from family disagreements over priorities. Some of these are so serious that they should be worked out in therapy. Most families, however, will find that, with the sources listed here, they can do a competent job by themselves. Since children also are consumers, it may be helpful to include them in deliberations. This not only gives them an idea of the value of money but makes them feel like an important part of the family and may increase their sense of responsibility. One family worked out an excellent scheme for doing just that.

> **Case 5:1.** Deputy Chief Thomas Granahan, of the East Orange, New Jersey, police department, and his wife, Ann, have six children. As each child reached the age of thirteen or so, Mrs. Granahan, who is the family's financial planner, sat down with that child and taught him or her how to write the checks to pay the family bills and balance the family checkbook. These tasks then became that child's responsibility (under the mother's supervision). These children know the cost of running a household and are much less likely to ask for extravagant items. The children also have a say in vacation planning: the amount of available money is announced, and they may decide whether to "blow" it all in the first days and go home early or to conserve and have a longer stay.

Physical Fitness

Chapter 1 talked of the interaction between stressors and physical state, especially the hypothesis of a relation between stress and physical illness. Some who write about stress and police have made a connection between physical fitness and stress, saying that poor physical condition is both cause and symptom of stress (Collingwood, 1980;

Hageman, Kennedy, and Price, 1979; Price, Pollock, Gettman, and Dent, 1978). These authors believe that a person in poor physical condition is less able to deal with other pressures, while people in good physical shape are better able to deal with the physical by-products of stressful events.

Some companies in the private sector also believe in the importance of physical conditioning and have instituted programs, often on company time with company facilities. They report generally improved health and some decreases in sick time (Linscott, 1981).

Despite police candidates' having to pass at least minimum standards of physical fitness to be appointed and recruit training programs' having a physical fitness component, policemen as a group are in no better shape than the average male and are in worse shape than fire fighters or prison inmates (Price et al., 1978). Older officers in Price's study were particularly high on factors considered as risks for coronary disease.

While there is evidence that people who participate in a regular, balanced program of physical exercise are less prone to coronary disease (Morris et al., 1973; Cooper et al., 1976), the link between physical fitness, reactions to potentially stressful life events, and psychological well-being is less clear.[7] Young and Ismail (1976) noted that adults who exercised a great deal were less anxious, more relaxed, more stable, and more confident than inactive ones, while DeVries and Adams (1972) found exercise significantly more effective than tranquilizers in reducing anxiety.

Price and his colleagues (1978) found that a physical fitness program brought some decrease in anxiety only in officers who were very anxious at the start and that there were no other alterations in psychological states or traits as measured by standard psychological tests. However, when asked directly about reactions to the program, the officers in the program reported that they were less tired and slept better than before. Some also reported greater overall job satisfaction and less worry about non-health-related matters, and 25 percent said their sex lives had improved. The wives of these officers echoed their reports.

Requirements for a Physical Fitness Program[8]

Fitness programs are often begun with a bang of enthusiasm and end, a few days later, with whimpers of pain, exhaustion, and disillusionment. Wisdom counsels those who are out of shape to get a thorough physical examination before starting any program that involves a major change in exercise or diet and then to start slowly.

Fitness is more than bench pressing 200 pounds. A comprehensive program includes adequate rest, weight control, and nutrition, as well as exercise.

NUTRITION. The authors know of no studies of the eating habits of police officers but have no reason to believe that they are better than those of the average American, which is a nutritionist's nightmare. Of particular interest is the contention that the physical changes associated with stress affect the body's ability to metabolize cholesterol.[9] Foods high in saturated fats, therefore, should particularly be avoided by people who are under continuing stress. Hageman, Kennedy, and Price (1979) further assert that refined flour, white sugar, caffeine, and alcohol stimulate the pancreas to produce more insulin, which in turn sets off a reaction similar to that of the general adaptation syndrome in that production of adrenaline and thyroxin is increased.

The basic principles of nutrition are taught in health classes in most public schools, and literature on the subject is readily available from one's own physician or the local health department; they will not be repeated here. Because so many know at least the rudiments of these principles but so few follow them, this again raises the issue of motivation. One factor that decreases the motivation of many to give up a diet that is generally considered unhealthy is the common experience that such a change leads to side effects such as headaches, irritability, and diarrhea, in effect, withdrawal symptoms. Hageman, Kennedy, and Price (1979) acknowledge these, but suggest that with a "cold turkey" approach the symptoms will be of short duration.

A recent phenomenon has been the appearance of over-the-counter medications touted as stress relievers. Some even claim to be especially for police and are advertised in police magazines. Most of these are simply high-potency vitamin and mineral preparations at an inflated cost. The same compounds are often available under generic names at discount drugstores.

An adjunct to nutrition is weight control. Many police departments consider excess weight to be a serious problem; of the 302 police agencies who responded to a survey by Price and his colleagues (1978), 60 reported having weight maintenance programs. In contrast to programs for overall fitness, most of which are voluntary, the majority of the weight programs are mandatory.

Although the evidence continues to show that gross obesity decreases life expectancy, the effects of moderate overweight are less clear (Bennet and Gurin, 1981). It is probably better to be a consistent ten pounds overweight than to lose on crash diets only to regain (Mazza, 1981). Indeed, there is no good evidence of the consistent long-term success of crash or fad diets, and some have proven harmful. Bennet and Gurin believe that the only way to lose weight and keep it off is through changing the body's metbolism; the safest way to do this is through daily exercise.

EXERCISE. Many physical fitness programs emphasize muscle strength. In reality, physical fitness also encompasses endurance and flexibility. How important each of these components is to an officer depends in part on his assignment: muscle strength is less important for those whose jobs are primarily sedentary than for those in more active assignments. Indeed, Price and his colleagues (1978) found that most police work involves little physical activity. However, endurance and flexibility are considered important for all officers.[10] Again, it is important to repeat the caution against overdoing any exercise program and to reemphasize the importance, especially for those over forty, of a physical examination before starting.

Before any extended exercise, a warm-up period of stretching, mild calisthentics, and the like is recommended. These are particularly important for the officer whose only physical exercise is the department's monthly softball game.

Weight lifting is the most common means of developing muscular strength. This is best done under supervision and is much less important for the average officer than are exercises for endurance and flexibility.

Endurance exercises increase the capacity of the heart and lungs; they make the heart beat faster during exercise, lowering the resting heart rate. The heart, thus, does not have to work as hard and is more efficient. Endurance exercises include running, walking, swimming, bicycle riding, jumping rope, and the like.

Exercise 5:3. A simple test for endurance.
Take your normal resting pulse. Exercise vigorously for five

minutes, take your pulse, then wait one minute. Take your pulse
again. An indicator of level of cardiovascular fitness is the speed
with which your pulse returns to normal after exercise. At the end of
one minute, the pulse rate should have dropped at least ten beats.
The quicker the rate drops after exercise, the better the endurance
(Hageman, Kennedy, and Price, 1979).

Flexibility exercises — stretching and bending — are particularly
good for the back problems that plague many officers. Price et al.
(1978) report that back trouble accounted for 16 to 23 percent of the
early retirements in the departments they canvassed. One program
that includes a rather complete complement of flexibility exercises is
that of the Royal Canadian Air Force, which is available in paper-
back book form. Any library has books that give similar regimens.

Officers with whom the authors have worked have added other
tips to help with back problems. Many of these involve avoiding
spending long periods of time with one's legs straight. For the officer
in a patrol car, they suggest driving with the seat pulled far enough
forward so that the knees are bent.[11] It is also wise to get out of the
car and stretch as often as possible. For long periods of standing, one
knee should be bent and supported on a rail or step.

A second set of suggestions involves the placement of uniform
equipment. Cuffs worn in the middle of the back when one does a
great deal of driving throw the spine out of alignment (as does a
bulky wallet in a hip pocket); they are better worn on the side opposite the weapon. Placing the gun high above the hip bone and
eliminating the second gunbelt also are recommended.

REST. Many officers complain of chronic fatigue, a problem exacerbated by rotating shifts. They also report difficulty falling
asleep. Some people find the relaxation and meditation techniques
that will be described later are helpful. Following are several other
gimmicks for those with this complaint.

Exercise 5:4. Gimmicks for dealing with insomnia.

Many people spend sleepless nights lying in bed worrying about
their inability to go to sleep. The worry itself, of course, feeds the
sleeplessness. The following gimmicks work to avoid that.

Gimmick 1. Assume you get in bed at 11:00. If you are still awake
at 11:20, get up. Pick some task that should be done but that you
loathe, such as preparing your tax return or cleaning the oven, and

spend twenty minutes on it. It is now 11:40. Get back in bed. If you are still awake at 12:00, get up again and return to your loathesome task. Continue this routine throughout the normal six or eight hours you would have spent in bed. Many people find they go to sleep to avoid the unpleasant task; at the very least, they have a sleepless night and a completed tax form.[12]

Gimmick 2. In a variation of gimmick 1, if you find yourself still awake after a half hour or so of lying in bed, get up and take some mild exercise, such as stretching exercises or even a walk. If it will not disturb others in the house, you might try listening to soothing music while you lie in bed, again to take your mind off worry about sleeplessness.

Gimmick 3. Some people bore themselves to sleep. Deputy Chief Tom Granahan of the East Orange police department tells the story of having chronic trouble sleeping during the many years he worked the midnight shift. On his night table he kept a copy of *Romeo and Juliet*. He read the first scene of the first act hundreds of times and never got further. As a variation on this theme, some people watch the television and bore themselves to sleep with the early morning reruns of old movies.

Gimmick 4. The relaxation and meditation techniques that will be discussed later in this chapter help some people get to sleep.

Several books aimed specifically at law enforcement officers are available for those seriously interested in physical fitness programs. The report by Price, Pollock, Gettman, and Dent (1978) is easily read and very specific in its suggestions. Its discussion of the legal aspects of fitness programs is particularly helpful for administrators.

Programs that encourage group participation are sometimes an aid in motivation. A police department team that participates in a community bowling or softball league not only is getting exercise but also is giving the public an experience with officers outside their official role.

Meditation

Relaxation, it would seem, is the antithesis of stress. In the past ten years or so, several specific exercises that are said to allow one to relax at will have become popular. One set of these is classified as meditation. Although there are many different types of meditation, those that have received most attention — attention that often has been uncritical — from laymen and from scientists are those that involve

> learning to direct one's attention toward a "mental device" (Benson, 1975) or a focus with which the student becomes passively absorbed. A variety of mental devices such as mantras (a special word or syllable), chants, prayers, visual symbols, or one's breathing or heart beat are used in various meditation techniques. Their function is to reduce or eliminate conceptual thinking ("the mental chatter") and to facilitate the development of an encompassing focus on the present moment and concomitant feelings of calm and relaxation (Seer, 1979).

Of these, transcendental meditation (TM), promoted by Maharishi Mahesh Yogi and popularized by such celebrities as the Beatles, is the best known. Indeed, much of the early research that showed such promising results was conducted under the auspices of his organization.

Many benefits have been claimed for meditation, among them reduced arousal, revitalized coping abilities, "a more balanced outlook and increased energy for dealing with whatever difficulties we are faced with" (Woolfolk and Richardson, 1978), the curtailment of obsessive thinking, anxiety, depression, and hostility, improved concentration and attention, help in spontaneous problem solving (Davis, Eshelman and McKay, 1980), and a global claim of "making behavior more orderly and life supporting" (Maris and Maris, 1978). Of particular importance are the claims that meditation decreases essential hypertension (high blood pressure) (Benson, 1975) and the diseases associated with it: myocardial infarction, congestive heart failure, stroke, and damage to kidneys, eyes, and other organs (Seer, 1979).

Others have been less sanguine and have pointed out methodological problems in the studies that occasioned optimism. Chief of these problems was that they failed to control for the placebo effect: subjects expected to improve. Smith (1976), Zuroff and Schwartz (1978), and Boswell and Murray (1979), with better controlled studies, found that meditation did not decrease either psychological or physiological measures of anxiety. Goldman, Domitor, and Murray (1979) concur, adding a finding of lack of improvement in perceptual function. These studies, however, observed subjects for only a short period of time, too short, perhaps, to see much effect.

In a review of the literature on the effect's of meditation on essential hypertension, Seer concludes that "most experiments demonstrated blood pressure reductions too small to be of clinical significance" and that the common component the techniques share of having the subject sit quietly for fifteen to twenty minutes a day may account for much of the effect that has been found. However, he believes that the various techniques are not equally effective for all problems and personalities and hopes that future research will allow "prescriptions" appropriate to the conditions. Given this, he expresses hope that relaxation and meditation will eventually be proven effective in the control of hypertension. He believes these techniques hold more promise than biofeedback because, unlike it, they do not require a sophisticated technology and because they have been reported simultaneously to reduce other stress-related complaints.

One of the most vituperative critiques comes from Stroebel (1982).

> There have been reports that TM leds to an increased incidence of various types of headaches, and some physicians have begun to report cases of long-time meditators developing serious side effects characterized by very frightening experiences. According to these reports, someone who has meditated for too long at one time may experience what has been described as mental lightning — flashing light accompanied by pain shooting up the spine and into the head. This phenomenon, referred to as "northern lights" or "aurora borealis," is called *kundalini* energy in Yoga, and there is a whole school of Yoga devoted to developing it, but under guidance and within a spiritual framework, so that it does not cause negative symptoms. People trained in TM who meditate a lot and have this experience have not been taught how to deal with this "unstressing" side effect.
>
> But the major problem with all three passive meditation techniques is that people don't stick with them after they lose contact with their instructors or training groups. Transfer of training from the structured learning situation to the outside world is not effective. The passive meditation techniques require two twenty-minute practice periods a day in a quiet room, away from the stresses of life. They apparently work as long as one keeps practicing, but people soon stop taking the time to practice (pp. 102-103).

Unfortunately, Stroebel does not identify the source of his first contention, so one cannot gauge how long "too long" might be or how frequently these effects had been found. Certainly, in this case, "too long" is much longer than the ten- to twenty-minute periods recommended for stress management. These side effects were not mentioned by Seer or by Murray's group; thus, although the present authors present them in a desire for completeness, they assume they are rare. Of course, anyone experiencing headaches or other unpleasantness would do well to discontinue meditating. The senior author has also heard of one incident in which a meditator had the hallucination of being outside of her own body. Again, this is an experience some people attempt to achieve, and it is probably frightening primarily because it is unexpected and not understood.

The charges of problems in remaining motivated, which are common to most of the techniques for stress reduction, are better founded and more serious. In fact, motivation — and expectation of benefits — may, as stated earlier, be the key to success. Thousands of people in this country have been trained in meditation (Maris and Maris, 1978) and have practiced it with pleasure and without ill effects.[13]

For those who wish to try meditation, the following variations on the technique developed by Benson (1975) are presented.

Exercise 5:5. Meditation.
The basic exercise is done as follows:
1. Find a quiet place where you will not be disturbed. Sit in a comfortable position. (It helps if you have support for your head.)
2. Close your eyes.
3. Relax all your muscles.
4. Breathe through your nose. Become aware of your breathing.
5. As you breathe out, say the word "one" silently to yourself. They rhythm goes like this: breath in . . . out, "one;" in . . . out, "one"; and so on. Breathe easily and naturally.
6. Do not worry about whether you are successful in achieving a deep level of relaxation. Maintain a passive attitude and allow relaxation to occur at its own pace.
7. When distracting thoughts occur, do not dwell on them, but let them pass out of your mind and return to repeating "one." Similarly, if you have an itch or tickle, take care of it and return to your routine.
8. Continue for ten to twenty minutes. You may open your eyes to check the time, but do not set an alarm.
9. When you finish, sit quietly for a minute or two, at first with

your eyes closed and later with your eyes opened. Do not stand up for a few minutes.

10. Meditate once or twice a day, but not within two hours after a meal.

Expect it to take several days to a week or more before you feel any results. You might also want to try variations on the basic exercise. One such variation is to pick a word other than "one": Davis, Eshelman, and McKay (1980) suggest using "in" while inhaling and "out" when exhaling, but other single-syllable words or even a nonsense syllable will do. Or, omit the word and just concentrate on the breathing.

Progressive Relaxation

Another form of relaxation makes the practitioner aware of tension in muscle groups and works on the principle that a muscle which is held very tense will automatically relax in a short period of time. To demonstrate this, clench a fist as tightly as possible and hold it. You will soon find that it begins to tremble. Progressive relaxation, as this technique is called, has, like meditation, been said to diminish all sorts of psychological and physiological problems that are believed to be stress related (Woolfolk and Richardson, 1978), including anxiety, and chronic headache and backache. It is also frequently used by behaviorists and cognitive behaviorists as part of a program to help clients rid themselves of phobias, of obsessive-compulsive behavior, and of anxiety (Coleman, Butcher, and Carson, 1980). It forms part of the cognitive behavior modification techniques discussed in the next chapter. The usefulness of progressive relaxation as an adjunct to therapy has been fairly well demonstrated (Kennedy and Kimura, 1974; Wolpe, 1969), but it has excited much less research than meditation, and its success as a self-help technique is still in question.

In the authors' experience, this form of relaxation, with its similarity to isometric exercises, is somewhat more acceptable to many action-oriented men than is meditation. Exercise 5:6 is presented for those who wish to try it.

Exercise 5:6. Progressive relaxation.

General instructions. First, read the instructions over to yourself several times so that you get the basic purpose and rhythm of the exercise. In the instructions, ellipses (. . .) mean a pause. Also, where the instructions say, "Hold it,. . . hold it,. . .hold it," the position should be held for about seven seconds. Many people find it helpful to tape-record these instructions, or to have a friend do it for them, and to play them back to themselves at first. There are also several tapes available from commercial sources. In time you will learn to relax without the tape. Do not hurry.

You may use the relaxation technique by itself or in connection with cognitive rehearsal, which will be discussed at length in the next chapter. The instructions will tell you where to insert this. For the time being, use the following mental device in this spot: Think of a calm scene, one in which you are alone, that makes you feel happy and relaxed. Many people find that a mental picture of the beach or the woods fits this qualification. Imagine you are turning on a video cassette recorder and playing this scene over and over as often as you like — one to five minutes generally is good. When you are ready, turn the set off.

Before beginning. Find a comfortable place where you will not be disturbed. You may either sit or lie down. Loosen any restricting clothing and remove glasses or contact lenses. If you find your mind wanders during the exercise, do not worry, just notice it and return to the exercise. You also may find that at first you feel nervous and have a tendency to laugh. This, too, is common and will stop in time.

Relaxation technique. Close your eyes and begin by inhaling deeply and exhaling slowly . . . inhale deeply and exhale slowly. Now tense the muscles of your head, face, and jaw and neck; clench your teeth and tighten your mouth. Hold it, . . . hold it, . . . hold it. . . Relax. Relax the muscles of the head, face, and neck and feel any tension that was there draining out of them. Inhale deeply and exhale slowly.

Now go to the muscles of the shoulders, chest, and upper back. Tighten them as hard as you can. Hold it, . . . hold it, . . . hold it. . . Relax. Relax the muscles of your shoulders, chest, and back and feel all the tension draining out of them. Inhale. . .exhale.

Go to your hands and arms. Hold your arms out in front of you and make a fist of your hands. Clench them as tightly as possible. Tighten all the muscles of your arms and hands. Hold it, . . . hold it, . . . hold it. . . Relax. Let your arms drop down by your side or into your lap and imagine that all the tension is draining out through your fingertips. Inhale deeply . . . exhale slowly.

Now all the tension is gone from your upper body. Move to your stomach and suck it in as hard as you can; tighten the muscles of your stomach and abdomen. Hold it, . . . hold it, . . . hold it. . . Relax. Just let go, and let all the tension drain out of these muscles. Inhale . . . exhale.

Go to your buttocks, and tense these muscles. Hold it, . . . hold it, . . . hold it. . . Relax. Inhale . . . exhale. Feel comfortable and relaxed.

Tighten your thigh and calf muscles and your feet. Hold them as tightly as you can. Hold it, . . . hold it, . . . hold it. . . Relax. Inhale . . . exhale.

Breathe deeply and slowly and enjoy the feelings of deep relaxation as you relax all the muscles in your head and face, in your jaw, . . . neck, . . . shoulders, back and chest, . . . in your arms, . . . your hands, your fingers. Relax the muscles in your stomach and abdomen . . . your buttocks. Relax the muscles in your thighs, . . . your calves, . . . your ankles and feet, . . . your toes. Relax the muscles in your entire body.

Now turn on the television set in your mind that has the cassette of your scene in it.

[Insert rehearsal here.]

That's fine. Now turn off the machine and continue to relax for the next few minutes. Feel relaxed, comfortable, and calm. When you are ready to get up, count "one" and take a deep breath. Count "two" and stretch your arms and legs. Count "three" and open your eyes and move your body. Now you are ready to go back to your normal activity.

Biofeedback

Another relaxation technique that has been suggested as a tool for stress management deserves mention here. This is biofeedback, a technique in which the subject is trained to control such supposedly involuntary reactions as muscle tension, sweating (the galvanic skin response), heart rate, finger temperature, even brain waves. As an example of the way this works, a subject will have sensors attached to the forehead that monitor tension in these muscles. He will

hear a tone (or see a light on a screen, or any number of other stimuli may be used) and be told that the tone reflects the tension state of
his muscles: when it gets higher the muscles become tenser, and it
will lower as they relax. He will be told to try to make the tone lower.
Many subjects can learn to perform these tasks in the laboratory.

Biofeedback has been suggested for stress management by police
(Axelberd and Valle, 1978); however, the authors believe its usefulness is very limited. First, the equipment is expensive, and someone
must be trained to administer it. Furthermore, although results are
equivocal, the bulk of recent research seems to show that effects are
generally small and may not generalize outside the laboratory, in situations where biofeedback equipment is unavailable (Blanchard and
Young, 1974, Holroyd, 1979). It has been found to be equal to or
less effective than relaxation training; when it does work it may be
because subjects have learned to relax or to change their ways of
thinking and of viewing the world, effects that can be achieved
without the use of expensive equipment (Holroyd, 1979; Lynn and
Freedman, 1979).

Support

The importance of social support and of ventilation were discussed in Chapter 1. Police officers need support from several
sources. First, they need the support of other officers; when an officer is in a crisis caused by a job-related incident, he usually finds it
helpful to ventilate to another officer who has had similar experiences. One form of ventilation mentioned frequently by officers
with whom the authors have talked was some version of what Wambaugh (1975) popularized as "choir practice" and which others call
"debriefing." These occasions usually were informal, often spur of the
moment, as events dictated. A group of officers from the same unit
or shift get together after work and talk about the events of the day.
In one unit, beer and pizza would be brought into the station for
end-of-tour parties (in violation of rules but with the tacit approval
of the unit commander). Members of the group felt these gatherings
solidified the group.

Unfortunately, if this form of ventilation is not carefully controlled, it can bring about disaster, as Wambaugh (1975) shows. Too
often the setting is a local bar, where alcohol and weapons are mixed

with outsiders. Thoughtful officers recognize these dangers, and several have told us they pick a spot across the county or state line, make sure they get a room to themselves, and leave weapons at home. One group said they take along a nondrinker to do the driving. In one case a chief, Richard Clement of Dover Township, New Jersey, (a former president of the International Association of Chiefs of Police) allowed officers to bring beer into the station house and drink it together at the end of the tour. If these occasions are carefully controlled, they can provide an appropriate setting in which officers can fulfill their need to ventilate.

Another source of support is the family. While many officers are loathe to take the job home and even may be warned about doing so in training, most wives want to know about their husband's joys and frustrations on the job (Niederhoffer and Niederhoffer, 1978).

A final support network is nonpolice friends. Many officers complain that civilians criticize their job. They fail to realize this is a peril of many jobs: physicians, attorneys, dentists, psychologists, teachers, and other professionals all bear the brunt of public gripes.

Wambaugh (Dreifus, 1980) summarizes the importance of support this way:

> [My personal life wasn't torn apart by the job because] I had a very good home life — simple as that. People going into police work should consider such things. They should ask themselves, "What kind of personal relationships do I have aside from police work, because I will need support?" Cops need good strong marriages, too. One thing's for sure, if you have a marginal marriage, police work isn't going to help. At any rate, you must have people you can relate to who are police officers, if you are to survive psychologically, but it's a mistake to band together with other police officers exclusively. . .
>
> . . .when policemen band together they tend to reinforce each other's paranoia. All the bad forces of police work are reinforced. I wish cops could go elsewhere — to civilian friends, loved ones, psychiatrists, psychologists, anyone who could help them. You need people to say, "There, there, there. You're seeing the worst of people and ordinary people at their worst. Your vision is distorted. The lens has to be cleaned. There, there, there" (pp. 36-37).

Summary

This chapter has presented a jumble of techniques for stress management, with some of the evidence about the effectiveness of each. The time- and money-management schemes are for specific problems; the fitness and relaxation techniques are more general, and more widely applicable. None in itself is a panacea, but each, followed faithfully but with moderation, will probably increase one's sense of well-being. The person who feels stress is a real problem for him will probably want to try combining several. Or, he may decide to seek professional help.

NOTES

1. This does not mean that such a goal may not be included in modified form, e.g. "Do what I can to give my children the opportunity to meet appropriate marriage partners." Specific steps in support of this goal might be, "Offer to help my daughter finance a weekend at a resort where there are rumored to be many eligible men," or "Get information for my son on groups that work on shyness." However, remember that a parent's control in these areas is severely limited. A son may be perfectly content with a limited social schedule.

2. The authors lack clear evidence on how common these feelings are in the general public or among police officers.

3. The major sources for the section on time management are Lakein (1974) and Davis, Eshelman, and McKay (1980). The section touches only the outlines of the techniques. Anyone who wishes to become seriously involved in an effort at time management would do well to consult these books.

4. At one time the senior author used the time spent in meetings which were required, but which yielded no useful information, writing letters to her grandmother or making up her "To Do" lists (on legal pads, so as not to attract undue notice).

5. Money, of course, is an issue that in our culture carries much emotional baggage: the self-worth of many people is dependent on how much they earn. Such people believe that money or material goods will bring happiness or that they deserve what they consider the good things in life. These issues will be dealt with in Chapter 6.

6. These agencies are listed in the phone book, or a directory of them is available from the National Foundation for Consumer Credit, Inc., in Washington, D. C. This directory also is reprinted in Ungaro (1980).

7. Few of the studies relating fitness to disease or to reactions to life events are well controlled, so the specter of the statistical truism that correlation does not imply causation again surfaces. For example, it may be that people who voluntarily, even eagerly, undertake exercise and fitness programs are in some other ways different from those whose greatest exertion is opening the garage door. It also should be noted that much of the research on the relationship of stress and physical fitness in police comes from an organization, the Institute of Aerobics Research of Dallas, Texas, with a vested interest in physical fitness.

8. Officer Robert Benthien of the Union, New Jersey, police department provided much of the material for this section. Lieutenant Andrew DiElmo of the Millburn, New Jersey, police department gave practical suggestions for dealing with back pain.

9. The link between dietary cholesterol and heart disease is not so clear as we have been lead to believe. Consumer Reports (1981), in a review of the evidence, states that "some scientists believe that . . . wide individual differences among people make blanket dietary advice concerning heart disease inadvisable for the general public. They argue that any decision about changing the diet of healthy people should await the outcome of studies not in progress.

10. Material in this section is drawn primarily from Price et al. (1978), Collingwood (1980), and Hageman, Kennedy, and Price (1979).

11. One complaint officers make about the suggestion that they drive with the seat forward is that they were taught to push it far back for pursuit driving. Although this may be appropriate in such a case, the high-speed chase is very rare for most officers, and a chronic backache hardly seems an appropriate price for vigilance of this sort.

12. The senior author learned the essence of this gimmick from psychotherapist Jay Haley.

13. A comment from the senior author: she learned to meditate from Benson's book about five years ago. Although she has never practiced it regularly, when she does use it, she finds it helpful in a variety of ways. The trick of concentrating on breathing helps calm her when she begins to get upset in situations in which being calm is important, such as testifying in court or being stuck in traffic. It also helps her cut off unproductive worries. When she has trouble falling

asleep, she finds it sufficiently relaxing that, even without the normal amount of sleep, she feels refreshed the next day.

Chapter 6

TECHNIQUES FOR INDIVIDUAL STRESS MANAGEMENT II: COGNITIVE STRATEGIES

Introduction

A SET of strategies that individuals may use to deal with stress reactions is called "cognitive": they involve retaining thoughts and beliefs, developing different attitudes. The idea of a strong connection between psychological processes — "mind" — and physical states — "body" — has a long history in philosophy, psychology, and the public. It is seen in aphorisms such as the following:

> Man is not disturbed by events, but by the view he takes of them.
>
> — Epictetus

> There is nothing either good or bad,
> But thinking makes it so.
>
> — Shakespeare

> The power of positive thinking. . . .
>
> — Norman Vincent Peale

> If your stomach disputes you, lie down and pacify it with cool thoughts.
>
> — Satchel Paige

Much of the research on stress cited in Chapter 1 supports the belief that the mental processes psychologists call cognitions — thoughts, attitudes, and beliefs — are an intervening variable between the stimulus

135

of stressor and the physical and psychological states, the responses, that have been attributed to stress. Thus, many psychologists believe that the way one thinks about events can exacerbate or alleviate stress reactions (Lazarus, 1966; Meichenbaum, 1975; Ellis, 1975).

Richard Lazarus, one of the early investigators of the link between thoughts and emotions, has expressed the relationship between them this way:

> First, . . .cognitive processes determine the quality and intensity of an emotional reaction; and second, . . .such processes also underlie coping activities which, in turn, continually shape the emotional reaction by altering the ongoing relationship between the person and the environment in various ways . . . (Lazarus, 1979, p. 144).

Examples of the premise that it is the way we think about events that influences our reactions to them abound in everyday life. An event may be defined by several quality dimensions, for example, from good and bad or from challenging to threatening. It may also be seen as ranging in intensity from having a major impact to being virtually unnoticed. As an extreme example, most civilians caught in the cross fire view war as a bad event, a threat, and a major occurrence; however, people in the United States differed tremendously in their attitudes about the Soviet invasion of Afghanistan. Few saw it as having a major impact, at least immediately, on their lives. General George Patton, for whom war certainly had a major impact, said of it, "God help me, I love it." For a less extreme example of attitude, one officer may see the promotion over him of someone he thinks is less worthy as a disaster, the end to his career hopes, while another may take it more philosophically; a third officer, who was ambivalent about promotion and took the test at the urging of others, is somewhat relieved not to have the extra responsibility. The first officer is the one most likely to display stress reactions.

Lazarus's second principle is seen in the self-fulfilling prophecy. If a cynical officer (sometimes called "Old Commander") believes all civilians hate the police, he is likely to treat them accordingly; his belligerent behavior (his coping strategy) probably will increase the hostility he receives in return. Sometimes, of course, the reactions of others make it very difficult to maintain a good attitude: "Dudley Do-right," smiling with universal trust and goodwill, may find it difficult to keep his sanguine belief in the goodness of all people and the ultimate triumph of the law when patrolling a beat in the heart of a major city.[1]

Kobasa and Maddi (quoted in Pines, 1980) are specific about the kinds of thoughts that exacerbate or alleviate stress reactions. In studies of the incidence of life stresses and illnesses among business executives, lawyers, army officers, and retired people, they found that

> stress-resistant people have a specific set of attitudes toward life — an openness to change, a feeling of involvement in whatever they are doing, and a sense of control over events. In the jargon of psychological research, they score high on "challenge" (viewing change as a challenge rather than a threat), "commitment" (the opposite of alienation), and "control" (the opposite of powerlessness) (pp. 35-36).

A relatively new method for helping people change their behavior relies heavily on making specific changes in the way they view themselves and the world. This method, or, rather, set of methods, has been grouped together under the heading of cognitive-behavioral therapy. While there is, of course, diversity among theorists who cluster under this term,

> two main themes seem to characterize them all. . . : (a) the conviction that cognitive processes influence both motivation and behavior, and (b) the use of behavior-change techniques in a pragmatic (hypothesis-testing) manner. That is, the therapy sessions are analogous to experiments in which the therapist and client apply learning principles to alter the client's cognitions, continuously evaluating the effects that the changes in cognitions have on both thoughts and outer behavior (Coleman, Butcher, and Carson, 1980, p. 650).

The cognitive-behaviorists differ from other schools of therapy in that they believe in the importance of changes in both thought *and* behavior and work with clients on both dimensions. They are aware of the findings of social psychologists (Gergen and Gergen, 1981) that attitudes are not necessarily directly related to behavior. One study of police, for example, shows little relationship between racist statements and differential treatment of the supposedly despised group. Another point should be raised here: It is fashionable to believe that attitude change must precede behavior change, expressed in the catch phrase "You cannot legislate the hearts and minds of men." However, social psychology gives equal weight to the idea that if people are encouraged to behave a certain way, their attitudes will change correspondingly (Festinger, 1957), supporting the maxim "Get them by the throats and their hearts and minds will follow."

Three of the cognitive-behavioral strategies that have been used widely in stress management are the rational emotive approach developed by Albert Ellis (1958, 1973, 1975), the cognitive restructuring therapy of Aaron Beck and his colleagues (Beck, 1979), and the self-instructional training of Donald Meichenbaum (1975), Raymond Novaco (1977), and others.[2]

Rational emotive therapy (RET) is one of today's more widely used therapeutic approaches (Garfield and Kurtz, 1976). It rests on a belief that problems in living stem from irrational, unrealistic beliefs about others and demands on oneself. There are certain "red flag" words that commonly indicate irrational thinking and that tend to bring on the physiological reactions of stress,[3] including "should," "ought," "must," "horrible," "awful," "worthless," "always," "all," "never," and the like. Ellis contends that stress reactions will be reduced if phrases such as "These people should respect me," ("or else," goes the hidden assumption, "I am worthless, because one should be loved by everyone for everything he does") are replaced by more moderate ones such as, "It is nice to have friends, but it is unrealistic to expect everyone to like me. However, it will be more pleasant for me if I can find ways to minimize conflict with these people."

One way to bring about change is to identify and dispute such thoughts. For example, one phrase heard many times from police is, "I hate this job, it's ruining my family, but I can't leave it." This may contain elements of the beliefs that "it is horrible when things are not the way I would like them to be," and "we have virtually no control over our emotions and cannot help having certain feelings," and "happiness can be achieved by inertia and inaction." The complainer might be asked why he feels he *cannot* leave the job. A typical answer is, "I have too much money invested in the pension." He might then be asked whether he knew of any other officers who had left the job in the same situation and what he would do if he were laid off. At this point he might admit that there was a positive reason for staying and that if things were really bad it would be worthwhile to give up the pension for the sake of his family. He would be led to the more reasonable statement, "There are some things about this job I find inconvenient and unpleasant, but on the whole, it is the best option I have right now." Next he might be encouraged to see that his attitude about the job has more to do with his family turmoil than the job itself, thus disputing the irrational belief that "human misery is produced by external causes, or outside persons, or events rather than by the view one takes of these conditions."

Beck also helps clients discover false beliefs. He is particularly interested in what he calls "automatic thoughts," those semiconscious things we say to ourselves about ourselves that led to self-defeating behavior.[4] Rather than debate his beliefs with the client, however, Beck would have him gather information about himself through unbiased experiments that serve to disprove the false beliefs. In the preceding example, the officer who feels trapped might decide with the therapist that one way to check his beliefs would be to talk with former officers who had left for other work or to see an employment counsellor. Together therapist and client would evaluate the information gained and use it as a basis for convincing the client to change his destructive thought patterns.

Self-instructional training, also called stress-inoculation training, has people work very specifically not only at changing the ways they talk to themselves but also at practicing using the new thoughts and observing their effects. Typically it has three phrases: education, rehearsal, and application. In the educational phase, therapist and client explore the client's maladaptive thought patterns and generate new ones that are less stress producing. For example, a client who becomes very anxious when taking tests may report that his self-talk includes statements such as, "I know there will be questions I haven't studied for, and then I'll panic, forget everything, and fail!" More realistic statements might be, "When fear comes, just pause. Keep the focus on the present; what is it you have to do? Take a deep breath and concentrate on the questions one at a time. Don't think about the fear; you can reason the fear away. It will be over shortly." Then the client rehearses these phrases. Finally, he practices using the techniques he has learned to decrease stress reactions, particularly panic and anger. This is done first with laboratory stressors, such as electric shock, or with role play in simple situations that arouse only minor upset. As the client is successful, the situations are made more stressful and more realistic.

A type of stress inoculation has been used to help police officers control severe anger. Novaco (1977) was interested in helping "the officer in mitigating his own anger and directing his behavior toward constructive resolution of provocative exchanges."[5] He, too, used a three-stage approach.

In the cognitive preparation stage, officers were given a framework for understanding anger; the importance of cognitive processes was stressed. Participants were encouraged to contribute examples of situations that provoked them to serve as a base for discussion. Some of these included a drunk who vomits in the back seat of one's cruiser, a citizen who refuses to help an officer who needs it, suspensions that are unfair, name calling, and the like.

For the skill acquisition and rehearsal phase, participants were divided into small groups, asked to describe in detail situations that provoked them, then asked to serve as consultants to each other to find useful ways of handling the situation.[b] The leader then lectured on the use of cognitive self-control skills, and coping self-statements were presented. For this, the idea was presented that provocation must be broken down into a series of steps and stages, with appropriate statements for each one. Examples of these stages and statements follow.

Examples of Anger Management Self-Statements Rehearsed in Stress-Inoculation Training[*]

Preparing For A Provocation

This could be a tough situation, but I know how to deal with it.

I can work out a plan to handle this. Easy does it.

Remember, stick to the issues and don't take it personally.

There won't be any need for an argument. I know what to do.

Impact And Confrontation

As long as I keep my cool, I'm in control of the situation.

You don't need to prove yourself. Don't make more out of this than you have to.

There is no point in getting mad. Think of what you have to do.

Look for the positives and don't jump to conclusions.

Coping With Arousal

Muscles are getting tight. Relax and slow things down.

Time to take a deep breath. Let's take the issue point by point.

My anger is a signal of what I need to do. Time for problem solving.

He probably wants me to get angry, but I'm going to deal with it constructively.

Subsequent Reflection

a. Conflict unresolved

Forget about the aggravation. Thinking about it only makes you upset.

Try to shake it off. Don't let it interfere with your job.

Remember relaxation. It's a lot better than anger.

Don't take it personally. It's probably not so serious.

[*]From Raymond W. Novaco, A Stress Inoculation Approach to Anger Management in the Training of Law Enforcement Officers, *American Journal of Community Psychology, 5(3)*:339, 1977. Reprinted by permission.

b. Conflict resolved

I handled that one pretty well. That's doing a good job!

I could have gotten more upset than it's worth.

My pride can get me into trouble, but I'm doing better at this all the time.

I actually got through that without getting angry.

The mere rehearsal of self-control skills, however, is not generally very effective (Meichenbaum, Turk, and Burnstein, 1975). For best results, one should have "regulated exposure to provocative situations in which these skills can be practiced" (Novaco, 1977, p. 340). This was done through role playing, conducted in small groups, again using participants as observers to provide support and feedback. The use of videotape also was suggested.

Although this approach seems promising, Novaco, unfortunately, is vague about the actual implementation of the program. He does not tell us the number of officers participating, the circumstances of their participation, i.e. were they volunteers or were they required to participate and, if required, was this because they had had problems? Furthermore, he provides no data on success of or problems with the program. A follow-up to assess whether the officers were willing and able to use these skills in real situations would have been particularly helpful.

The effectiveness of any therapeutic technique is difficult to determine for a number of reasons (Garfield and Bergin, 1978), but the early studies of the effectiveness of cognitive-behavioral methods are promising. Mahoney and Arkoff (1978) report that self-reinforcement procedures have demonstrated consistent effects over a wide range of populations and behaviors. Specifically, they have been used successfully in the treatment of depression (Beck, 1975), headaches (Holroyd, 1979), asthma (Ikemi et al., 1982), and social isolation and schizophrenia (Meichenbaum, 1975). They have even been used to increase creativity (Meichenbaum, 1975). Furthermore, these techniques have been found superior to those oriented only toward cognitions or behaviors (Fuchs and Rehm, 1977; Shaw, 1977; Taylor and Marshall, 1978).

Despite these promising results, or perhaps because of them, we must take care to avoid what Birk (1974) has called "furor therapeutics." It is common for a new therapeutic technique to be greeted with enormous optimism and fanfare, including a frenzy of optimistic publications. Critical evaluation, time, and new therapeutic fads

put a damper on the initial enthusiasm.[7] Therefore, the early promise of cognitive-behavioral methods for stress management is still
subject to empirical scrutiny and revision.

In particular, Coyne (1982) warns against seeing thoughts as a
cause of behavior unlinked to the reality of what is happening to the
person, especially to feedback from the environment. For example,

> it is often found that [depressed persons] have some basis for negative
> self-perceptions. Depressed persons are inept in task performance, they
> prove aversive and get rejected in conversations with strangers, and
> their relationships with others are characterized by strain and interper-
> sonal conflict. . . . (p. 9) [references deleted].

Thus, thinking "I really know how to do this job" when basic skills
are lacking is of little long-term value when the person gets constant
evidence of his ineptness. Coyne points out, also, that the person
must believe the thoughts the therapist presents. He gives further
evidence that change in behavior which leads to change in feedback
can influence thoughts.

Already a number of books translating the principles of
cognitive-behavior therapies into self-help strategies have come on
the market. The best of these the authors have seen are *Stress, Sanity
and Survival* by Woolfolk and Richardson (1978), *The Relaxation and
Stress Reduction Workbook* by Davis, Eshelman, and McKay (1980),
and *Thoughts and Feelings: The Art of Cognitive Stress Intervention* by
McKay, Davis, and Fanning (1981). Although these books have
some basis in theory and are generally sensible and easy to follow,
they present little specific data to support their claims that these tactics, undertaken on one's own, will reduce stress reactions.

Even if the early promise of change under therapeutic guidance is
fulfilled, it does not necessarily follow that this success will transfer
to self-help measures. Again, motivation is the issue; while
cognitive-behavioral methods perhaps lend themselves to self-help
better than many other change strategies, the support of a therapist
and the pressure that comes from having paid substantial fees to get
help may be an important variable in producing change.

Irrational Thought Patterns

All of the cognitive strategies described so far rest on the belief
that certain patterns of thought, which are largely irrational, mediate stress reactions. They hold that erroneous ways of viewing the

world keep people from effective problem solving. These beliefs often are not well articulated or part of a person's full consciousness; it takes a bit of self-analysis and probing to uncover them.

None of the people whose work is quoted would recommend a life devoid of emotion. They suggest, rather, that the emotion should be appropriate to the situation. Thus, a traffic jam or a slur on one's ancestry are appropriate causes for mild, controllable irritation, but not for rage.

The authors take the liberty here of combining the ideas of a number of theorists, including Ellis and Harper (1975), Beck (1979), Woolfolk and Richardson (1978), and Farquhar and Lowe (1974), to present some of the most common of the thought patterns considered irrational and harmful.

1. *Worry, by itself, prevents mistakes and misfortunes, helps anticipate the future, or gives one added control over the course of events.* Many people lie awake at night worrying about money, for example, but fail to make a budget or speak with a counsellor. Many also have had the experience of getting a message that the boss wants to see them. People immediately assume the worst and may be so nervous by the time they walk into his office that they confess all transgressions only to find that he needed some minor piece of information.

Worry tends to be self-perpetuating and self-escalating, feeding on itself. Once we begin to worry, we tend to overestimate the importance of the feared event. We think that one false move or one uncautious word has ruined our chances for happiness. Soon we find ourselves worrying because we worry so much and working ourselves into what our grandmothers would have called a "snit."

> **Case 6:1.** Captain Eric O'Malley was serving as watch commander when one of the department's officers made a felony arrest of a man who was running for political office in the town. The man was convicted, but the case gained national publicity. The man was given executive clemency and released. Now he is charging a number of the members of the department, including Captain O'Malley, with false arrest. O'Malley worries about this constantly, to the extent that it is affecting his sleeping and eating; he has the beginnings of an ulcer, and his family life has deteriorated. He envisions himself in

> prison, his career gone, and his family on welfare.
> However, he has done nothing to assess realistically
> the chances that an indictment will be returned
> against him; for example, when he talked with the
> senior author about his problem, he had not spoken
> to an attorney. (The attorney to whom we sent him
> believed that the likelihood was very small; indeed,
> it was virtually unknown for an indictment for false
> arrest to be returned in that state.)

In one situation worry may be helpful: if worry leads us to prepare for the most likely of the possible outcomes of a situation, it is useful in that we understand them and have a framework in which to place them. Janis (1965) found that people coped better with the stress of surgery if they had spent time before thinking about it, preparing for and rehearsing it, and planning for contingencies. Burstein and Meichenbaum (1974) found similar results with children who were surgical patients. Lazarus (1979), however, believes that denial is the most adaptive response to situations beyond our control.

2. *Grousing and feeling sorry for oneself will somehow magically prevent disaster or make things better.* The reality is that they have few benefits in the long run and seem mainly to encourage procrastination. Chronic griping is at almost epidemic levels in some police departments; indeed, it seems to violate some unwritten code of the organizational culture to admit publicly to liking the job.[8]

3. *Thoughts, by themselves, have the ability to affect the physical environment or other people.* Many people believe this, but "wishing will not make it so." Magical wishes for elevators to appear, lights to turn green, traffic to move (spurred on by frantic honking), mayors to evaporate, beautiful women to fall effortlessly into one's arms, errors to disappear, and the like are largely a waste of time.

People often torture themselves with useless questions such as, "Why doesn't the lieutenant go play in traffic?" "Why don't these creeps just go away and leave me alone?" "When is this organization going to give me what I deserve?" "How could this have happened to me?" Woolfolk and Richardson (1978) suggest that people should either learn not to ask themselves these questions or get into the humbling habit of answering quickly and move to something more important.

A corollary to this is the belief that because one thinks something is so, or someone else says it is so, it must be so. The number of men who get upset over comments about their manhood, their maternal ancestry, or their wives' occupations is truly remarkable; if such remarks are as unfounded as the recipients claim, why get upset? Police officers, who are particularly likely to be the targets of such comments, are in no way immune to such provocation.

4. *It is absolutely necessary for an adult to have love and approval from everyone for everything he does.* While most people find that their lives are richer and more satisfying if they have people who like them, and whom they like as well, it is impossible to please everyone all the time. Even people who are friends will find some behaviors and qualities in each other that upset or annoy them. Furthermore, no relationship can give a person a feeling of security unless he is secure in himself — witness the tragedy of Othello and others whose unfounded jealousy made their lives miserable. Although people often deny this belief, they become upset at any slight, any criticism, or any sign of disagreement or difference of opinion.

5. *One must be unfailingly competent, intelligent, and achieving — almost perfect — in everything one undertakes.* Expecting oneself to be perfect leads to inevitable failure, tension, and self-loathing. Perfectionists often procrastinate, to the point of becoming paralyzed with fear at the idea of attempting something new; they think it is better to do nothing than to make a mistake and thereby reveal their worthlessness.

Many people who set unrealistic standards for themselves regard themselves as permanently disadvantaged compared with others. They get a perverse pleasure from playing the game of "You think *you* have troubles." They use the idea of their disability as an excuse for not achieving the standards they have set: "If only I were (or were not) stuck in this job/marriage/town, were rich/lucky/younger, I could be happy/get ahead/find someone to love me. Everyone else has it better than I do. Just look at Jerry; he gets all the breaks."

Perfectionists are particularly likely to see every sphere of life as a series of contests won by the good, pure, and righteous. They evaluate themselves by their successes. Since no one wins them all, people who hold these beliefs are constantly vulnerable to threat and irritation.

6. *Others must also be perfect.* This expectation leads to blame,

anger, and disappointment. Intolerance leads to moralistic thinking about how others should or should not behave. Many come to believe that people who disappoint or hurt them are doing so because of malice or because of a basic character flaw. People who hold this belief spend much time trying to find someone — usually someone else — to blame for their misery.

7. *One must have certain and perfect self-control.* This is another form of perfectionism. There also is a fallacy current in our culture that says that a person can be anything he wants to be if he only tries hard enough. Accidents do happen, and forces outside people's control do influence the course their lives will take. For example, a person may be over forty years old and under six feet tall. Even given unlimited time, effort, and money, and the best possible trainer, it is highly unlikely that he could attain a goal of becoming a linebacker for the Pittsburgh Steelers. A Nobel Prize in physics also is outside his grasp if he has only a high school education.

8. *Happiness consists of unremitting idleness.* Giving up perfectionism does not mean going to the opposite extreme of inaction, self-indulgence, laziness, and sloppiness. Included here are the ideas that happiness can be achieved by inertia and inactivity and that it is easier to avoid life's difficulties and responsibilities than to face them. Avoidance of some difficulties may be the best course in some situations, however, especially when one has no control over them or they involve trivial matters. Certainly it relieves anxiety in the short run, but for most problems, avoidance creates more stress than it removes.[9]

9. *Human misery is produced by external causes, or outside people or events; people simply react as events trigger their emotions.* This is the antithesis of fallacy number 7; neither of these extremes is rational. This notion leads to the fatalistic belief that people can have little control over themselves and cannot help what they feel or think. The research cited earlier in this chapter, however, has demonstrated that such control is possible for many people in most situations.[10]

10. *It is horrible when people and things are not as we would like them to be.* People who believe this think they have the right to be eternally free of inconvenience and discomfort and always to get their way without effort. This person has a low tolerance of frustration.

11. *We are totally ruled by the past.* This fallacy has received unfortunate support from analytic psychologists and psychiatrists, who

have convinced many of us that our lives are ruled by childhood experiences. We use ghosts that inhabit our pasts to escape responsibility, as blame for our present problems. Recent research (Bruner, 1978) questions this assumption. Although change may not be easy, it is possible.

It often is helpful to remind oneself that the past is over; nothing can be done to change it. Worrying about it can certainly do nothing but increase unhappiness. Thinking about the past is useful only when it leads to plans for avoiding mistakes in the future.

While some people spend their time regretting things that have happened to them in the past, others yearn for "the good old days." They compare their present lives with inaccurate memories of past times and regret real, or often imagined, losses. This keeps them from looking for pleasure and challenge in the present. They fail to see that the "good old days," viewed realistically, had their own problems. Diseases that were common only a few decades ago, polio, tetanus, diptheria, tuberculosis, have all but disappeared. The majority of the officers with whom the authors have worked will admit to having far more in the way of material possessions than their parents had at the same age.

12. *If something is unknown, uncertain, or potentially dangerous, one should be terribly upset about it.* People are often paralyzed by fear of the unknown, sometimes preferring an unhappy certainty. They stay in jobs and relationships in which they are miserable because of fear of this sort; the battered wife at least knows what to expect. They "rehearse . . . scenarios of catastrophy, . . . [thereby] increasing the fear or anxiety . . . [which] makes coping more difficult and adds to stress" (Davis, Eshelman, and McKay, 1980, p. 106).

13. *Other people will change to suit us if we pressure them enough.* People who believe this spend their time whining, moaning, and making others feel guilty instead of dealing with their own behavior and taking responsibility for themselves. While occasionally others will change, resentment and counteraggression — either passive or active — are more likely results.

14. *Life should be fair, and if it is not, that is intolerable.* The belief in a just world, where people get what they deserve and deserve what happens to them, is common (Lerner and Miller, 1978). Acknowledgment of the reality that the world is often unfair is as old as the biblical story of Job. Indeed, the definition of fairness often is sub-

jective; two parties in a conflict, working by different rules, usually have entirely different ideas about what is fair. Anguish over the unfairness and inequality of the world is often seen in the talk of police officers; they complain about inequities in everything from promotions to the release of a suspect before the officer's paperwork is finished.

15. *Overgeneralizing* is a kind of irrational thinking in which a global conclusion is based on very few pieces of evidence. For example, a subordinate who is criticized by a supervisor once may get the idea that, "He hates me. I'll never get any place in this job." Overgeneralizations tend to be statements that include words such as always, never, all, every, none, everyone, or nobody.

Alternative Ways of Thinking: Guidelines for a Low Stress Life-style

The cognitive approaches to stress management give examples of adaptive thinking styles to counter the irrational thought patterns described previously. They suggest that when a person finds himself engaging in inappropriate thinking, he should substitute more adaptive thoughts and behavior consistent with these thoughts. Of course, this will take time and effort. Some exercises to facilitate this process will be presented later in this chapter. Although these are touted for the relief of pressure, Coyne (1982) injects a note of caution, pointing out a lack of support in the literature for the efficacy of some of these techniques, such as thought stopping. He reiterates the importance of changes in behavior as well as changes in thinking.

The following list of alternative ways of thinking is in part the antithesis of the irrational thoughts described earlier. For it, the authors have drawn largely on Woolfolk and Richardson (1979) but also include suggestions made by officers in the stress management courses they have taught.

1. The first maxim of stress management, as mentioned earlier, is to have *the serenity to accept what one cannot change, the courage to change what one can, and the wisdom to know the difference.*

2. From the first proposition, it follows that *a person can and should learn to accept both his personal shortcomings and his lack of control over much of what will ultimately happen to him.* This involves giving up perfec-

tionism and learning to tolerate one's own frailties. It suggests looking realistically at one's own possibilities and limitations. The average officer cannot, alone, significantly reduce crime, put all felons in prison, or change the court system. He can, however, do the best investigation possible, act in a professional manner, and so forth.

3. *Acceptance of shortcomings should be accompanied by realization of strengths.* Many police officers denigrate their jobs and themselves. For example, they are unhappy in the job or are facing retirement from the force but want another job. They ask themselves, "What am I fit for? I'm only a cop." While it is true that technological skills such as lifting a latent fingerprint have limited applicability in the civilian world, a broader analysis of the job and the necessary skills shows that officers have experience in dealing with people in crisis and in making quick decisions in difficult situations. These skills do generalize and can be made highly marketable.

4. *Happiness cannot be achieved when pursued as a goal.* Happiness is never sought or achieved directly. It is always a by-product of other activities. Happiness usually results from stopping the focusing on oneself and becoming absorbed in other activities. Furthermore, money and material possessions do not bring lasting happiness. Organizational psychologists (Herzberg, 1968) tell us that money may keep us from being miserable, but it does not make us happy. Police officers frequently say that if they had more money from their job they would not moonlight. The authors doubt this and think it much more likely that their needs and expectations would rise to the level of their income — or beyond. Anecdotes of the "poor little rich" person abound; recent research shows severe problems of adaptation among children of top corporate executives (Burke and Bradshaw, 1981).

Many officers adopt a fatalistic unwillingness to take responsibility for their own unhappiness: they blame the bosses, the politicians, anyone but themselves, and deny that they can do anything about their fate or their misery.[11] While it is indeed true that they have limited control over outside events, they can, cognitive theorists remind us, control the way they think about them.

To counteract this tendency to blame everyone but oneself, Tom Granahan (who was mentioned previously) reminds his students that "you can only bloom where you are planted." Everyone needs to take ultimate responsibility for his own happiness. Although people need some things from others, no person can make another happy and secure. While the approval of others is desirable, it is not necessary.

5. *It is important to learn to laugh* — at oneself and occasionally at the world in general — in a benevolent, unhostile way. A sense of humor not only brings relief from tension but helps in self-acceptance. This is one of the more positive of the defenses in crisis.

6. One should accept that *the struggles of life change; they never end.* It is well for a person to stop waiting for the day when "he can relax," or when "his problems will be over." That day will never come, and if money is important, there will never be enough. Most good things in life are fleeting. Savor them. It is a waste of time to look forward to the "happy ending" of all troubles.

7. *Life often will be unfair,* and there is little sense in being surprised and shocked when something unfair occurs. Also, believing that one has a right to be free from discomfort or that one deserves to get everything one wants produces a low tolerance for life's frustrations. This is not an endorsement for adopting a fatalistic attitude, however, nor is it an excuse to mistreat others. One should simply try to arrange the world around one so that it will be as fair as possible as often as possible.

8. *A low stress life-style typically is reasonably efficient and well managed.* Laziness, self-indulgence, and sloppiness usually create more stress than they remove.

9. *The past is over*; there is nothing anyone can do to change it. Because ruminating on the past is a very common cause of pressure, it is important to repeat that thinking about the past is helpful only if it leads to plans for avoiding mistakes in the future. Worrying about the past is never helpful. Pasts are inhabited largely by ghosts that are of little use in present life. These ghosts are often circumstances that are used as excuses for inadequacies, parental standards that are goals for achievement, or inaccurate memories of the "good old days." To focus largely on the past is to rob the present of its joy and vitality and to keep one from looking for challenge and pleasure in the only time one can control — the present (Woolfolk and Richardson, 1978).

10. *An antidote to worry is asking "What is the worst thing that could happen if my worries become realities? How likely is this to happen? What can*

I do about it?" This helps put the situation into perspective.

11. *One should find something other than oneself and one's achievements to care about and believe in.* Selye (1978) believes that the greatest of all modern stresses is purposelessness.

Some people get a sense of purpose from doing a job that they believe is intrinsically worthwhile. For others the source of purpose comes from religion. There is evidence that people with a strong religious faith, regardless of denomination, are less susceptible to damage from stressful life events than are those with more tenuous beliefs; indeed, regular participation in religious services, even if one's belief is not strong, helps alleviate pressure — perhaps because of social support. Anecdotal support for this proposition comes from the American embassy personnel who were held hostage in Iran from 1980 to 1981: many of them reported that they had prayed together and read their Bibles daily. Other evidence of the importance of a broad philosophical view of the universe and of human nature comes from reports of survivors of Nazi concentration camps (Frankl, 1962).

One of the advantages of policing as an occupation is that police are a crucial agency in our, or any, society, and they do make a difference to people. This is a particular advantage of the service role; as many observers of the police have pointed out, people come to the police when they are in need, and the police are uniquely suited to providing crisis intervention (Bard and Ellison, 1974; Cumming, Cumming, and Edell, 1965; Brodyaga et al., 1975).

Changing Thoughts and Behaviors: Exercises

This section will present some simple exercises for the do-it-yourselfer. They may also be used as class exercises in stress management courses. These exercises are not the answer to every complex problem in living. Although there are anecdotal reports that they have worked for some people, the authors know of no solid scientific evidence either supporting or refuting their general effectiveness.

Since many of the cognitive-behavioral strategies derive from the individual's goals, the first step is to return to Figure 5-1 on page 108 and review — or do — the exercise it presents.

Exercise 6:1. Stress diary.[12]

1. During the next week, keep a diary of situations that were stressful to you, ones in which you felt annoyed, bothered, irritated, or upset. Briefly, describe when the incident occurred, who was present, what the setting was, how you felt, what you said to yourself about the event (your thoughts), what you said to others and what you did, and how upsetting (on a scale of 1 to 100) you found this incident. (This rating will be referred to as SLD, for subjective level of distress.) A form for this diary may be found in Figure 6-1.

Stress Diary

Day/Time	Situation	Feelings	Thoughts	Actions	SLD

Figure 6-1.

Examples of entries might be as follows:

Example 1.

Day/Time: Mon/0920

Situation: On traffic duty. Driver, 22, refused to move on, told me to mind my own business.

Feelings: Anger

Thoughts: How dare he? I'll show him! (If I don't it would mean I'm not a real man.)
Actions: Cited him for everything I could find. No registration; had car impounded.
SLD: 50

Example 2.

Day/Time: Wed/1540
Situation: Asked lieutenant for change in day off so could go to wedding.
              Refused — said not enough notice.
Feelings: Rage
Thoughts: That bastard! How dare he? I'll show him
Actions: Told him what I thought of him. Got one-day suspension
SLD: 75

2. At the end of the week, look over your list and see if you can find a few general categories in which a number of these stressful events can be placed. You do not need to be too precise or compulsive about this; just see if some common themes emerge. Some examples might be (1) interactions with civilians in which your authority or masculinity is called into questions, (2) interactions with superiors or peers in which your competence is questioned, (3) evaluations by others in general, (4) situations in which others seem to be unwilling to accept responsibility, (5) close relationships, (6) competition. Write down common themes as they occur to you. Notice common themes in the column "thoughts." For help in this, go back to the section on irrational thoughts beginning on page 142.

In the stress diary excerpts presented, an underlying thought seems to be, "I must have my way all the time, with no inconvenience, or my masculinity is threatened." Anger is the common emotion followed by overreaction.

Exercise 6:2. Refuting irrational ideas.

Exercise 6:2 follows from Exercise 6:1. Pick one situation of moderate SLD and analyze it using the following worksheet. For Alternative Thoughts, review page 148.

Worksheet for Refuting Irrational Ideas

Activating Event:

Irrational Ideas:

Consequences of the Irrational Ideas:

Disputing and Challenging the Irrational Ideas:

1. Select an irrational idea.

2. What evidence is there that this idea is false?

3. Is there any evidence that this idea is true? How strong is that evidence?

4. What is the worst thing that could happen to me —
   a. in this situation?

   b. if I think about the situation in a different way?

5. How bad is the worst thing that could happen?

6. What good things might happen?

Alternative Thoughts:

Alternative Feelings/Emotions:

Plan for Action (Problem Solving):

An analysis of example 2 from Exercise 6:1 might go like this:
Activating Event:
   Refused permission for wedding.
Irrational Ideas:
   I have a right to be free from inconvenience.

If anyone disagrees with me, it must mean I'm unworthy. (I must be liked by everyone, etc.)

I cannot control my feelings or temper.

Consequences of the Irrational Idea:

Rage, overreaction, which got me into trouble. I had plans for that money I'll lose.

Disputing and Challenging the Irrational Idea:

1. I cannot control my feelings, temper.
2. I have learned not to get sick at accident scenes.
   Other people don't get so angry in similar situations.
3. No, just because I've had trouble controlling my temper in the past doesn't mean I can't change.
4. (If I had accepted it calmly, and not blown up): I don't get to go to the wedding. I am disappointed, and feel frustrated. I've had much worse things happen to me.
5. I'll try asking earlier next time.

Alternative Thoughts:

This is inconvenient, but I can survive it.

I can try another approach — go over his head.

Getting upset won't do me any good.

How can I prevent this inconvenience in the future?

What can I do to help me control my anger in the future?

Alternative Emotions:

Annoyance, disappointment

Plans for Action (Problem Solving):

Talk to other people I trust about how they solved similar problems.

Set a specific time to read up and work on ways to deal with anger better.

Forget about it; it's not worth the hassle.

Exercise 6:3. Stress inoculation.

Assume you are in a situation that you expect to be stressful and that in the past has upset you and made you angry. This time you want to try to do things differently.

Step 1. Relaxation. Return to Chapter 5 on page 127, and review the Progressive Relaxation Exercise (Exercise 5:6).

Step 2. Review the stages and the coping statements from the Examples of Anger Management Self-Statements on page 140. Other appropriate statements might be as follows:

Preparation:

What's the worst thing that can happen if this doesn't turn out the way I want it to? How bad is that?

There's nothing to worry about.

I'm going to be all right.

I've done much harder things than this before.

What are some logical arguments I can present?

Impact and Confrontation:

Stay organized.

Take it step by step, don't rush.

I can do this; I'm doing it now.

I can only do my best.

It's all right to make mistakes.

Any tension I feel is a signal to use my relaxation exercises.

Coping with Arousal:

Take a deep breath.

No need to rush. Just stick to the point.

I can keep this within limits.

Just think about what I need to do.

Subsequent Reflection:

a. Conflict unresolved.

Well, you tried. Better luck next time.

What have I learned from this that I can use in the future?

I didn't get upset. I'll bet that surprised him.

b. Conflict resolved.

Now I have some strategies that seem to work. I can try them again in the future.

I did a good job that time.

Step 3. Make up other statements that may be appropriate to a logical way of dealing with the situation.

Step 4. Go through the progressive relaxation. At the point marked "insert rehearsal here" run through the stressful scene in your mind, playing it as if it were a video cassette. Use the calming statements you have generated in step 2. If you find yourself getting upset, switch back to the calming scene until you feel more in control. Then return to the stressful scene. Do this until you can get through the stressful scene without upset.

Step 5. If this is a very important situation, find someone with whom you can role play it.

Exercise 6:4. Thought stopping.

Thought stopping works on the theory that certain thoughts, in themselves, generate stress. It is the antithesis of the Freudian belief that a person must "get it out of his system." Thought stopping has been used therapeutically to deal with obsessive thoughts and fears (Lazarus, 1971; Rimm and Masters, 1974; Wolpe, 1969). The senior author has found that rape victims can use thought stopping very effectively to help deal with flashbacks and constant replaying of the scene.

Step 1. Start with a thought pattern that is only moderately upsetting. If you have the same upsetting thoughts frequently, you may find it useful to practice thought stopping out loud, by yourself, first. In this case, find a place where you can be alone and uninterrupted. Set a timer for two minutes, then start to think the thoughts deliberately. Continue thinking about them until the timer rings. Then say, loudly, "Stop." Take several deep breaths and say to yourself, "This isn't doing me any good, and I don't have to think about these things." Concentrate on your breathing for a minute. Then, if the thoughts return, reset your timer and begin again. Do this three or four times, increasing the time between thinking sessions.

Step 1a. An alternative to step 1 that sounds strange at first but which people have said works well is to put a thick rubber band around your wrist. When the obsessive or upsetting thoughts start, snap the band and say, "Stop," to them. (Yes, it hurts; that's the idea.)

Step 2. If thoughts are not very obsessive, or after you have gotten some success with step 1, you might want to try the same technique but instead of shouting "stop" out loud, try saying it to yourself.

Step 3. In place of the inappropriate thoughts substitute more positive, assertive statements.

Exercise 6:5. Dealing with worries.

If you feel you *must* worry but are spending so much time at it that you cannot get other things done, you might find this exercise helpful.

Step 1. Pick a time each day that you will set aside specifically to worry. Fifteen to twenty minutes should be enough.

Step 2. If you find yourself worrying at other times, use the thought stopping techniques described earlier and tell the worrisome thoughts, "Go away. I'll deal with you later."

Step 3. In the time you have chosen, sit down and write down all the worries from the previous day that you can remember. You will find that many of them have been forgotten, have been resolved, or no longer seem important. Go back over the list. For each one, ask yourself, "Is there anything I can do about this? What? Would it be worth the effort?" If the answer is no to any of these, take a ball-point pen and vigorously scratch the item off the list. When this worry arises again, remind yourself that you have chosen not to deal with it, and use the thought-stopping techniques, if necessary. If the answer is yes, draw up a plan of specific steps for dealing with the situation, and write them on your calendar or "To Do" list.

Summary

The techniques presented in this chapter may sound silly or frivolous. A cynical officer would be tempted to say, "I'm not going to do that (expletive deleted) stuff. I'd be embarrassed." The decision of how bad the stress is and how much one is willing to risk to try to alleviate it is up to the individual. In this, as in other areas of life, motivation is a crucial element. Furthermore, there is no 100-percent guarantee with these strategies; they are simply some of the things that seem to have worked in similar situations for other people. They are relatively benign: if they are not successful, the chances that they will do harm are small.

NOTES

1. Of course, there is a more rational alternative to either the "Old Commander" or the "Dudley Do-right" position. This is the person who does the best job he can, looks for ways to do it better, but realizes that there will always be elements he cannot control and, hence, that are not worth worrying about. This stance is exemplified by the homicide investigators described in Chapter 2.

2. With apologies to them and their disciples, the authors will combine the "irrational thoughts" of all these theorists later in the chapter.

3. "Red flag" is the authors' term, not Ellis's.

4. A common automatic thought among police who fear that they will lose face in an encounter either with a civilian or with others in policing is the pervasive thought, "You'll look like an asshole." This is, perhaps, the most common epithet in policing.

5. It is important to note here that Novaco did not find that police officers were particularly prone to provocation. He found that their anger responses did not differ from those of a sample of normal college males and in some situations were less prone to anger.

6. The technique of peer consultation used here is similar to that of the very successful model program developed by the Oakland, California, police department to deal with inappropriate aggressiveness in officers (see Toch, Galvin, and Grant, 1975).

7. It is instructive to remember that the technique of frontal lobotomy was touted as a panacea for behavior problems and even won a Nobel Prize.

8. Several times in stress seminars the authors taught, they have been approached during a break by an officer who almost sheepishly admitted that he "didn't want to say anything in there," but he really likes his work.

9. For a discussion of the relative merits of avoidance as a conflict resolution strategy, see Hampton, Summer, and Webber (1978) or Phillips and Cheston (1979).

10. The authors do not take this to the extremes that some of the writers do for a popular audience, whose books are based loosely on cognitive-behavioral theory. Some of these seem to say that external events are of no consequence and that the individual has total control over thoughts and feelings. Humans, as noted earlier, are social animals, and strict adherence to such a credo would allow administrators to shirk their responsibility, laying the blame for stress-related disorders and poor performance on the individual. More than one department has had an organizational climate such that competent policing was difficult if not impossible. Catch 22 lives in too many police settings.

11. This trait is not, of course, limited to police.

12. This section has drawn heavily on Woolfolk and Richardson (1978) and on the books by Davis and McKay (1980, 1981) for these exercises.

Chapter 7

TRAINING

Introduction

As information about an area such as stress is compiled, the task then becomes one of how best to pass on this knowledge — these skills — to those who need it most. As police departments and individual officers have become increasingly aware of the prevalence of stress-related problems in policing and their potential impact on efficiency, morale, and psychological and physical well-being (not to mention the problems of liability), training programs for stress management have proliferated.[1] Although much of the literature on stress has emphasized the importance of organizational structure and supervisory style in the prevention or exacerbation of stress-related disorders, most of the training and most of the programs have been aimed at the individual: at teaching the officer to recognize and deal with the symptoms of stress in himself.

Although the authors do not quarrel with the importance and sincerity of these programs, they feel that an effective program of stress awareness and management must include more extensive and comprehensive training. It must focus on changes at the organizational and supervisory level in addition to programs geared for individuals in the lower ranks. Particular problems arise when well-intentioned trainers teach skills that the department will not allow the trainees to use; when, for example, sergeants are trained to spot and counsel problem officers but are given no disciplinary control over them because someone higher in the hierarchy is protecting them (Daviss, 1982).

Real success in stress management involves changes at many levels, changes most departments will likely be unwilling to make. Certainly sending the department's worst discipline problems — the "burnouts," or, as the director of the St. Louis police academy calls them, the "crispy critters" (Daviss, 1982) — to a one-day seminar along with thirty or forty others will not solve the problem.

Evaluation of stress management training programs has been almost nonexistent. When it is done, it most commonly takes the form of asking for comments on the quality of the course at its completion. Some form of the question "Do you think this will help you in your work?" is often included. There is no evidence of any relation between this measure and any change in behavior. No objective measures of change, especially long-range change, either in attitudes *or*, more important, in behavior are taken. Admittedly, research of this sort is very difficult to do.

Stress management involves changing behavior; as such it encompasses a complex set of skills, skills that can seldom be mastered in a course lasting a day or even a week. The best that most courses in stress management can hope to achieve is to give administrators and officers a brief overview of the problem, to make available a few gimmicks whose main aim is to get people who are interested started and motivated. They can then suggest sources of information and help for those who wish to know more and do more.

Although the authors have given these caveats, they shall nevertheless describe a training program in stress management. This program was designed for academies that serve a number of jurisdictions; thus, classes have officers from several different departments.[2] This is a good arrangement because it allows officers to share experiences and successes with each other and to find that others have similar problems. It also strives to reach a relatively wide audience. However, it can, the authors believe, be modified to fit a wide range of situations and needs. Although the immediate response from students has been very favorable, there is a lack of external evidence that the courses produced change, either short or long range.[3]

A comprehensive training program might include the following elements:

1. An executive seminar for command level personnel.

2. Courses for first-line supervisors — sergeants and lieutenants, which would be of two types: (a) a segment on stress management could be included in the course in basic supervision that is intended to train newly promoted first-line supervisors; (b) an in-service course would acquaint supervisors who missed this in their earlier training with the area and would sharpen the skills of those who have some knowledge of stress management.

3. Courses for officers in assignments that have been found to involve especially high levels of stress. As in the courses for first-line supervisors, a section on recognizing and managing stress reactions could be included both in initial and in-service training.

4. In-service courses for patrol officers.

5. A section on stress in recruit training.

6. Courses for police spouses.

7. Preemployment courses for prospective officers.

The length of each course or section and the material covered will, of course, vary from jurisdiction to jurisdiction, depending on the nature of the jurisdiction and the severity of the problem, as well as on the available resources. The most severe restriction the authors have found has been on time. Thus, while the ideal course for chiefs would last several days, practical realities suggest that few chiefs, especially of smaller departments, will feel they have the time to devote to such a course, so a one-day format may be necessary if one's aim is to reach large numbers. In cases where there are severe time restrictions, the initial training can be limited to essential material, including an understanding of basic principles, other information provided through the use of extensive handouts, such as those in earlier chapters of this book, and follow-ups providing individual consultation for special programs and problems.

Another frequently mentioned excuse for not giving stress management training is lack of funds. The authors have found, however, that with imagination and flexibility, much can be done with very limited finances. Handouts, including audio- and videotapes, can be prepared; instructors can be recruited from local departments and from criminal justice training programs. Advanced graduate students and, in some cases, undergraduates with extensive experience can be invaluable here. Sometimes these students can be given credit for their work.[+] In addition, films may be available on interlibrary loan, and drama students from local colleges not only are excellent for role playing but are often pleased for the chance to practice their craft.

Note on Training Methods

In stress management, as in other skills that involve interacting with people, the best training involves a great deal of class participation and practice of the skills in the sheltered atmosphere of the classroom setting where feedback can be given immediately. However, the authors have found that police officers are particularly sensitive to a fear of ridicule by peers, so it takes special time and effort to encourage them to take an active part in the training. For example, attempts to demonstrate techniques such as meditation with large groups participating together must be undertaken with caution and may not work very well, especially if the course is short and most of the officers have not come voluntarily. The atmosphere tends to degenerate into uneasiness, heightened by gratuitous comments and laughter. The class is lost, and it is difficult to regain credibility.

In some courses, if the instructors cannot deal with participants individually in class, the best method is to give a relatively complete discussion of the various techniques and hand out prepared materials with simple instructions that can be followed on one's own. Materials of this sort appear in Chapters 5 and 6. The instructors also make active use of break time to single out individuals who appear to have questions or problems with the material but may be reluctant to ask questions before the group.

Frequently, important issues will arise, which are dealt with before starting the next section of instruction — giving credit to class members for good insights or suggestions. Indeed, the instructors try to be sure that at least one member of the staff speaks individually to each participant in this informal matter. They also encourage students to use their breaks to get to know members of other departments better, exchange information, and build a support network.

When there is more time, the staff find it best to build up trust gradually so that students feel comfortable admitting to problems. One tactic that has worked well as a starting point is the use of case histories. Sometimes the instructors provide these, sometimes, in a course lasting more than a day, the students are asked to generate them anonymously on the first day. The students are divided into groups of four to six and are given a case with questions to answer. The instructors emphasize that there are no right and wrong anwers, that the right answer will depend on one's goals and resources. The group is asked to come up with suggestions. Then the case and solutions are presented to the entire group, and their comments and additions are solicited. Examples of some of these cases will be presented later in this chapter.

Problems with participation are particularly acute when many officers in the group do not come voluntarily, but are sent. They wonder why they were chosen, tend to take it as a comment on their mental stability, and suggest that the boss who sent them should have come himself instead. It is very important to deal with this immediately and specifically, to say, "We know some of you did not come because of personal interest, but were sent. You may resent this. However, now that you are here, you have some choices. You can waste this time and go away feeling resentful, or you can make the best of it, and see if perhaps you can find something that can be of use to you. We acknowledge that we cannot force you to learn anything, but we hope, perhaps, we can exchange some ideas that will be helpful to all of us."

One commonly used training method is the use of pretest and posttest role playing. At the beginning of the course, officers role play a situation similar to that for which they will be trained. They are expected to do badly and thereby be motivated to learn. At the end of the course, there is another attempt at role playing, intended to show everyone how much they have learned. The authors disapprove of this technique. Occasionally the first role play will go well, and the trainer is left with egg on his face. If it goes badly, the officers who participated are humiliated in front of their peers, and everyone becomes afraid that participation will lead to similar humiliation. It creates an atmosphere that is seldom conducive to learning.

A much better way, the authors have found, is to start with lectures, demonstrations, and discussions, then go to simple situations and gradually lead into practice in more complex situations. The emphasis should be as much positive and as little negative reinforcement as possible.

One technique that has been very successful for role playing is to have outsiders, such as drama students from local colleges, playing the parts of civilians; officers only play themselves. We tell all officers taking part that they are to make at least two mistakes deliberately. They are to identify one for the class in the discussion that follows, but one they are to keep secret. This has several advantages. First, it allows them to make mistakes safely, without fear of ridicule; second, they may discover that the class did not pick up on the behavior they thought was glaringly inappropriate.

Curriculum Core

The core of all the training programs involves an understanding of the theoretical basis of stress and stress management and its special applications to police work.[5] It rests on the belief in the importance of cognitive variables: that stress management begins with the perception that one has some measure of control over some elements of one's life (as well as the willingness to recognize and accept that one cannot control everything) and a belief that such a perception is helped by understanding.

In the programs described here, the core section is team taught by one or more police officers and a psychologist who has worked extensively with police. The two or three teachers are "on stage" at the same time, and no one speaks more than ten or fifteen minutes at a time. This combination increases flexibility and ability to deal with questions on both a theoretical and practical level. As time allows, other instructors who are specialists in subareas of the core material are included.

The core material begins with a general introduction to stress theory and emphasizes the challenge, as well as the dangers, in stress. Next, the special stress factors in police work are discussed. Stressors external to the police organization are mentioned briefly but not dwelt upon because, while awareness of their impact may be helpful, there is little that officers or command personnel can do directly to change them. Much more time and emphasis, varying with the group, are given to factors over which that group does have some control: stressors in the organization for administrators, stressors in supervisory style for first-line supervisor, and stressors that come from personality factors for everyone. Although danger signals indicating an individual or organization at risk or already in the throes of stress-related problems are presented, emphasis is on a proactive, preventive approach. A variety of programs that have proved successful or seem promising are described.⁵ When at all possible, the course includes a speaker from a local group that provides peer counseling for officers with problems, particularly problems of alcohol abuse. This segment is largely lecture, with the inclusion of a film or two.

Whenever a competent instructor is available, the course includes a section on the legal implications of stress. Each group is told its rights and its responsibilities under the law: administrators and supervisors learn the legal expectations for vicarious liability and progressive discipline, and officers are told their legal rights. While this is crucial for administrators, it has been well received by all groups.

Next, participants are given the questionnaires from Chapter 3 to fill out in class. This usually serves as a break from lecture and motivates many of the students who find that they have many of the symptoms the questionnaires describe.

All groups also are given a presentation on physical fitness. The instructor for this comes from the academy or from a local department with a strong fitness program; in addition to lecturing, he shows a film and often demonstrates exercises. All of the courses' instructors have tailored these demonstrations to the average age of the class members, with special emphasis on flexibility exercises for middle-aged, sedentary administrators.

The next phase is a discussion and demonstration of the relaxation exercises. For reasons discussed earlier, unless the majority of the members of the class have volunteered to come, or unless the class has been unusually responsive, students are not asked to practice these in class. For the sake of credibility, this presentation is best given by an officer who is well thought of by the group. The exercises from Chapter 5 are given out as handouts for those who wish to try them.

Finally the instructors deal with the cognitive techniques. They give the goal-setting exercise described in Chapter 5 and follow with a short lecture on irrational thought patterns. At the beginning of the course, officers were asked to write anonymously examples of situations that they found stressful. If there is time, the class may now be divided into groups and given one of the incidents to analyze following the form for refuting irrational ideas in Chapter 6. Each small group then presents its case to the class, and the floor is opened for general discussion.

The class ends with a short summary presentation from each of the principal instructors emphasizing again the importance of personal responsibility for the areas one can control.

As mentioned earlier, programs for different ranks are tailored for that group. Some of these differences will be outlined in the following sections.

Command Personnel

As has been stated a number of times previously, a program must have the support of top management if it is to work well without tremendous upheaval. Because of the importance of organizational factors in stress, the authors believe the first, most important training program must be the one aimed at top management. If executive officers are unaware of problems and are unwilling or unable to make changes in management and supervisory practices that produce stress in large numbers of their subordinates, if, indeed, they encourage behavior that is officially condemned and protect certain officers whose actions are clearly inconsistent with official policy, programs aimed at the lower ranks can have, at best, only limited success.

Because of the magnitude and complexity of the changes that may be required to minimize stressors from organizational style, this program is also the most difficult. The instructors try to avoid giving too many simplistic formulae for change at this level. They concentrate, instead, on including diagnostic tools and suggestions for sources of help, should these tools indicate problems. In the authors' executive seminar for police administrators, they present management theory and give concrete examples of programs that have implemented this theory successfully. In this, it is particularly powerful to have representatives of several such programs present to describe their approaches and answer questions.

For administrators, the discussion of supervisory techniques often reiterates material from other courses or readings in basic police supervision. In this case coverage can be brief and can emphasize the dual importance of good supervisory practices both for increasing efficiency (about which they have already learned) and for managing stress.

At the level of the individual, selection procedures, personnel evaluation techniques, and ways of dealing with problem officers, including possible legal remedies in extreme cases, are discussed.' At this point it is necessary to reemphasize that such procedures are not a panacea, that even the most carefully selected officer cannot do his job well without support from the organization.

Finally, the instructors talk about the stresses command level personnel experience and, as mentioned before, offer suggestions for a variety of programs that participants can undertake for themselves with a minimum of equipment and supervision.

At least one of the police members of the team that teaches the core segment to administrators is captain's rank or above. Again, this is to give the best possible feeling of rapport and understanding between teachers and the managers who are the students. In addition to this team that teaches the core segment and the representatives of model programs, instructors in this course can include a psychologist or police manager who has specialized in police selection, an instructor whose specialty is teaching police supervision, a specialist in organizational development, and an attorney who is versed in the legal aspects of selection procedures and procedures for dealing with problem personnel.

SAMPLE CLASS SCHEDULES

Executive Seminar on Stress Management

One-Day Course

9:00 – 9:45 The nature of stress
9:45 – 10:30 Stress in policing
10:45 – 11:15 Recognizing stress in self and others
11:15 – 12:00 Management strategies for stress control
1:00 – 2:00 Model programs
2:00 – 3:30 Legal aspects of police stress
3:30 – 5:00 Personal strategies for stress management

Film: *The Silent Killer*

Two-Day Course

Day 1

9:00 – 10:00 The nature of stress
10:00 – 11:15 Stress in policing
11:15 – 12:00 Recognizing stress in self and others
1:00 – 2:30 Management strategies for stress control
2:45 – 5:00 Legal aspects of police stress

Day 2

9:00 – 11:00 Dealing with the problem employee
11:15 – 12:00 Model programs
1:00 – 2:30 Class exercise: Developing model policies
(see "Training Aids")
3:00 – 5:00 Personal strategies for stress management
Physical fitness

Film: *The Silent Killer*

Relaxation and meditation
Cognitive techniques

First-Line Supervisors

In the courses the author's team has given, they have consistently devoted the most time to the course for first-line supervisors. Much of their work with first-line supervisors consists of reemphasizing the principles of good supervision and their importance in stress management. They mention only briefly the stressors resulting from factors inherent in the police role and in organizational factors. They stress the importance of the supervisor as the street officer's basic contact with the organization and as a force for socialization, as well as the person first able to detect and deal with early signs of problems.

The instructors spend considerable time on factors that might cause acute crisis reactions in officers and discuss ways, at these times, the supervisor can reward good coping strategies or teach new ones or, in contrast, ways he can make the problems worse. Emphasis is placed on possible signs of distress in subordinates, and suggestions are made of nonthreatening ways of checking into them and of helping the officer cope with them should a problem emerge.

Of course, the instructors cover the special stressors inherent in the role of police supervisor and include the basic segment on recognizing and dealing with one's own stress reactions as best one can.

Teaching methods include lecture, films, and handouts, as well as case material from typical situations that confront supervisors. The team has had success with the use of group problem solving, emphasizing "What are our goals in this situation?" "What can we expect?" "What are our options?" "What outcomes are possible, and how likely and desirable is each?" and "How does this fit into what we have learned?" Examples of the cases we use are given later in the section entitled Training Aids. This exercise always proves to be a learning experience for us and confirms our respect for the basic skills of many of our police colleagues. It also provides those who are less skillful with a peer model and peer support and gives at least minor gratification to those whose hunches have proven right.

At this level, as well as at the one below it, the authors find it particularly helpful to include among the instructors at least one who has extensive supervisory experience in a department respected either for its professionalism or for the difficulty of the job of policing in that locale, or ideally both. It is preferable that this person be a sergeant or lieutenant; with higher ranks the rationalization is that "he has been off the streets so long he doesn't remember what it is like." Here, again, a team-teaching approach is valuable.[8]

SAMPLE CLASS SCHEDULE

Three-Day Course

Day 1

9:00 – 10:15 The nature of stress
10:30 – 12:00 Stress in police
1:00 – 2:00 Recognizing stress in self and others
2:15 – 5:00 Supervisory strategies for stress management

Day 2

9:00 – 10:45 Special problems:
            Accidental stressors (shooting, etc.)

      Film: *Dealing with Death*

      Alcohol abuse
      Other problems

11:00 – 12:00 Legal aspects of stress management
1:00 – 2:30 Interviewing and counseling the problem
 employee
2:45 – 5:00 Class exercise: 4
 Case studies (see "Training Aids")

Day 3

9:00 – 10:45 Class exercise
 Role playing
11:00 – 12:00 Personal strategies for stress management
 Physical fitness

 Film: *The Silent Killer*

1:00 – 2:15 Personal strategies (*continued*):
 Time management and financial planning
 Relaxation and meditation
2:30 – 5:00 Cognitive methods

Particularly Stressful Assignments

Perhaps the best way to give stress management to officers in particularly stressful assignments is to include it in in-service courses that deal with all phases of the assignment. As with training for first-line supervisors, it is best if the initial training precedes the assignment, but refreshers are also helpful.

While much of this training proceeds as does that for the individual officer, the unique stressors of the special assignment are previewed (or reviewed, as the case may be) so that the officer will not feel that he is the only one who is affected or that crisis symptoms are reflections on his manhood or his abilities as an officer. In this course it is crucial for at least one of the instructors to have had experience in the special assignment and, if he is not already known to the participants, to be able to gain their respect quickly. The selection of this instructor requires some care, as his support for the program and the practical advice and examples only such a person can give can make the difference between a program that is barely adequate and one that motivates the participants into commitment of the sort necessary to implement changes of the magnitude that such programs may suggest.

Patrol Officers

The literature is replete with reports of programs aimed at the individual officer (see Duncan et al., 1979). Programs for the lower level worker have been undertaken not only by police departments but also by industry. Some of these have been consistent with theory, others may most charitably be described as frivolous. In the latter group was a hobbies fair for employees of a large suburban county government, based on the idea that outside interests of this sort will, by themselves, alleviate tension in the work place.

The authors confess some reluctance to become involved in the training of patrol officers. They have been strong advocates for change at the organizational and supervisory level because they are concerned that the program which aims only at change in the individual is ignoring what are more potent factors in stress and is providing the potential for blaming the victim. For example, a department sends its "crispy critters" to a one-day stress seminar. They come back to the same environment that helped toast them but are told, with an air of great self-righteousness, "Look, we gave you all that time, and spent all that money to send you to that course. Now if you mess up, it's your fault." The authors believe that even the best, most highly motivated individual cannot function efficiently if the organization is not structured to support such functioning. In a maladaptive organization, the individual who will not feel stress often is the one whose major goal is to keep a low profile and do as little work as possible.

Individuals do, however, differ in their abilities to tolerate the stresses of the job; even in the best-run departments, some potentially harmful stressors will occur. Also, not all stress that affects an officer's work comes from the job; the potential for problems from a variety of accidental and nonaccidental events related to the job has been well documented in the literature on stressful life events reviewed in Chapter 1. Therefore, the authors have been persuaded of the importance of including training in stress management at the lowest level of the police hierarchy.

Here, as in the other programs, the team offers the core section. Officers often want to spend most of the time denying the possibility of any responsibility, and thus any personal remedy, by complaining about the court system, the politicians, the public, and the politics of the department. The instructors acknowledge the importance of these in their lectures, but their standard litany is, "You can only bloom where you are planted. There is little or nothing you can do about that (other than becoming involved in the political process, of course). You can only deal with factors you can control. What are they?"

As in other courses, the instructors give a variety of alternatives. They talk at length about the importance of physical fitness, including weight control and diet. They teach the basics of meditation and relaxation. They use the goal-setting exercise and teach the principles of cognitive change. They discuss the importance of retirement planning and suggest a hard look at the pension that keeps so many officers feeling trapped — or allows them to use it as an excuse. They put their best professional muscle into a reaffirmation of the value of the police officer.

Techniques include lectures, films, and group work using problem-solving techniques, with an emphasis on the creative use of war stories. Handouts are used copiously.

At this level, a sergeant, lieutenant, or top-grade detective is often most effective as the police instructor. Again, the tendency is strong either to feel reluctant to discuss problems with top brass, to feel that they have been away from the street so long that they no longer understand its problems, or to use the time as a free-fire gripe session.

Sample Class Schedules

Stress and Policing:
A Course for Patrol Officers and Detectives

9:00 –   9:30 The nature of stress
9:30 – 10:45 Stress in policing
　　　　　　　　Film: *Dealing with Death*
11:00 – 11:30 Recognizing stress reactions
11:30 – 12:15 Legal aspects of stress — employee rights and responsibilities
1:15 – 2:15 Personal strategies for stress management
　　　　　　　　Physical fitness
　　　　　　　　Film: *The Silent Killer*
2:30 – 5:00 Relaxation and meditation
　　　　　　　　Cognitive strategies

Recruit Training

Emphasis on the officer's feelings and reactions and on ways to deal with them while continuing to behave professionally should be a part of any role-playing exercises in which recruits are taught to deal with people. The recruit is told, in effect, "It is normal to have these feelings, but you can learn to control them. You do not have to act on them." In this way, stress management is integrated into the general curriculum.

For recruits, the content of a special course segment on police stress is much the same as for individual officers, with emphasis on the importance of understanding and prediction. Recruits are warned to expect crisis reactions to a variety of situations, are told ways to recognize the symptoms, and are assured that such symptoms are not necessarily signs of unworthiness. The preventive measures taught to recruits are the same as those for more seasoned officers.

A section on stress fits best into course material on crisis intervention and victimology, building on the principles learned there. The best instructors usually are seasoned officers with, perhaps, a carefully chosen psychologist or other behavioral scientist as a team teacher.

The Family

Courses for spouses and fiancé(e)s of officers are becoming increasingly popular, both for recruits and for veteran officers. The best are those that include both partners in the relationship and not only deal with the stress for the officer of his job but also help the officer see the special stresses the job may place on a spouse. Although likely to meet with fierce initial resistance from officers, programs that provide "ride along" experiences for spouses have proven successful where they have been tried.

Techniques include lectures, films, discussion, and demonstrations of relaxation and cognitive techniques. The wives of recruits can also benefit from very practical suggestions, including how to deal with the schedule. Demonstrations such as self-defense and firearms safety instruction may be included. Instructors for this course should be very carefully chosen. It should not be allowed to deteriorate into a session of griping and self-pity, as happened in one instance with which the authors are familiar. The best instructors for such a course are a team of an officer and his or her spouse and a psychological professional such as a marriage counselor.

Training Aids

FILMS. A number of films on stress are now available. Some of these are catalogued by Duncan and his colleagues (1979). The major flaw in many of these is that they are overly optimistic and simplistic; thus, the officers in the authors' courses have commented that they present a parody of the job. One film particularly escapes this censure: *Dealing with Death* (Motorola Teleprograms, Inc.) is a powerful movie and has been well received at all levels of the authors' training programs. It can be used at the beginning of a course as a source of discussion, in the section on stress and policing, or at the end as a summary.

Another film that has proved to be popular is *The Silent Killer* (Traveler's Insurance Co.). It gives the outline of a model physical fitness program and is also well received by officers of every rank.

CASE MATERIALS. As was mentioned earlier, the authors frequently divide classes into small groups and give them case histories to discuss and present to the class. Following are some examples of the cases the authors have used.

Development of Policy Statements (Executive Seminar)

Groups are asked to develop a model policy statement and a procedure for each of the following situations:

1. Dealing with officers who have been involved in shooting incidents.

2. Dealing with officers who have been severely injured in the line of duty.

3. Dealing with officers suspected of suffering from severe psychological problems.

4. Dealing with alcoholic officers.

5. Dealing with officers in very stressful assignments. Include any particular training or support services that might be necessary in these assignments.

Participants are asked to include special considerations for small versus large departments, rural versus suburban versus urban departments, and the like. It is a nice gesture for the trainers to edit these after the course is over and make them available to the participants.

Case Studies (Supervisors).[7]

Case 1.
I. Background.
    A. Personal information.
        1. Detective Len Stands, age 32.
        2. Appointed eight years ago.
        3. Wife recently died in a car accident; no children.
        4. Assigned to investigation unit for five years.
        5. Senior man in his unit.
    B. The situation.
        1. Stands has had several minor (almost trivial) complaints from victims of crimes he has been assigned to investigate.
        2. You have heard rumors that he is not paying attention to his work.
        3. His clearance rate for cases has recently been the lowest in the unit, although formerly it was the highest.
II. The problem.
    A. You are this man's immediate superior. You are under pressure from your bosses to keep productivity up. You know that there are many other officers in the department who have requested transfers to your unit. You have decided to interview Stands.
        1. What is the objective of your interview?
        2. What points do you want to cover? For each, tell why.
        3. What techniques and principles of interviewing will you use.
    B. Is there any additional information you would like to have before the interview? What? How will you go about getting it?
    C. What, if anything, might have been done to prevent this situation?

Case 2.
  I. Background.
      A. Personal information.
          1. Officer Josh Kozinski, age 45.
          2. Appointed twenty-one years ago.
          3. Divorced, has three children, ages 23, 20, 7.
          4. Average performer. Seems content with patrol duty, although he has taken the sergeant's exam several times and done poorly.
          5. Has had a reputation as a heavy drinker for many years. Frequently looking for someone to go out for a drink after work.
      B. The situation.
          1. In a routine review of sick leave, you notice that Kozinski has taken sick leave much more frequently than other officers. He is usually out for a day or two. This pattern began about six months ago.
          2. Although all the other officers state that they like Kozinski, in the past year two men who worked with him have requested new partners.
  II. The problem.
      A. What preliminary questions or assumptions, if any, might you make about Kozinski?
      B. What, if anything, should you do about this situation.?

Case 3.
  I. Background.
      A. Personal information.
          1. Detective Herb O'Reilly, age 36.
          2. Appointed twelve years ago. Six years as a detective.
          3. Married fifteen years; four children, aged 2 to 13.
          4. Religious, but not a fanatic. Easygoing. Likes the job.
      B. The situation.
          1. You are O'Reilly's supervisor. You have received a report of a particularly grisly homicide case involving a 3-year-old boy tortured to death, presumably by his parents.
          2. You assign O'Reilly to the case.
  II. The problem.
      A. What assumptions, if any, can you make about O'Reilly?

What problems, if any, might he have as a result of investigating this case? What is the likelihood of these problems?

B. Having made the assignment, is there anything you should do (aside from routine follow-up of the case)?

Case 4.
 I. Background.
  A. Personal information.
   1. Officer Alan White, age 21.
   2. Appointed six months ago, recently returned from academy.
   3. Single. Just moved into own apartment.
   4. The youngest man in the department. Very eager and enthusiastic. Older men like him but tease him about his age and about being "gung ho."
  B. The situation.
   1. As supervisor, you go to the scene of an auto accident. White is already there. Three people are badly injured, at least one is already dead.
   2. You know this is White's first DOA.
  C. What preliminary assumptions, if any, can you make about White? What problems, if any, might he have as a result of working on this case? What is the likelihood of these problems?
  D. What, if anything, should you say to him? When is the most appropriate time?
  E. Are there any other actions you should take?

Case 5.
 I. Background.
  A. Personal information.
   1. Officer Edward Heath, age 27.
   2. Appointed five years ago. Now on patrol duty.
   3. Married six years. Two children, one aged 4 years and one 14 months.
   4. Satisfactory record.
   5. Presently attending college. In his senior year.
  B. The situation.
   1. You have come to work early to catch up on paperwork.
   2. You get a call from the desk officer. He tells you that he

has just gotten a call from one of the radio units. They report that they have just found Heath and a civilian lying wounded on the street.

    3. A subsequent call from another unit on the scene reports that Heath has told them that he was on his way to work when he observed two young men trying to get into a store. He was driving his personal car and approached them. When he identified himself, one turned and fired at him; he returned fire. One of the suspects is badly wounded and may not survive. The other got away. Heath has severe cuts on the arms and seems to have injured his back. He is being taken to the hospital. His family has not been notified.

II. The problem.
    A. How will you handle this situation? (Forget about basic investigative chores for the moment and focus on crisis work with the officer and his family.)
        1. What steps should you take? When? Why?
        2. What will you say to Heath?
        3. What will you say to his family? Who should notify them? How?
    B. What sort of follow-up, if any, do you plan?

Case 6.
  I. Background.
    A. Personal information.
        1. Sergeant Joe Capoletto, age 31.
        2. Appointed eight years ago. Sergeant two years.
        3. Married, two children, another on the way.
        4. College degree in criminal justice; working on master's degree in public administration.
        5. Field supervisor in narcotics unit.
        6. Moonlighting (with permission) at two jobs.
    B. The situation.
        1. The lieutenant's exam is coming up in one month, and Sgt. Capoletto has announced that he plans to take it.
        2. In the month since the exam was announced, Sgt. Capoletto has been irritable and snappy with his men and with superiors. He has started coming to work looking tired and disheveled.

    3. His performance has deteriorated.

II. The problem.

    A. You are this man's superior officer.

    B. What, if anything, should you do about the situation?

Case 7.

  I. Background.

    A. Personal information.

        1. Officer Sam Peters, age 40.

        2. Appointed fourteen years ago.

        3. Performance very good.

        4. Married (wife is attractive); three children aged 9, 12, 15.

    B. The situation.

        1. Mrs. Peters has come to you, her husband's immediate supervisor, whom Officer Peters allegedly respects highly.

        2. She states that during the last two years Officer Peters has been chasing another woman, and his conduct is rapidly becoming a neighborhood scandal. She says that his conduct is such that the department will undoubtedly be embarrassed soon if something is not done promptly.

        3. Mrs. Peters has spoken first to your superior, who referred her to you. He tells you to do whatever is necessary to prevent possible embarrassment to the department.

        4. No complaints have been received by the department, and Peters's conduct, if factual, has apparently not affected his work.

        5. Neighbors have not been interviewed, nor have Mrs. Peters's allegations been supported by other evidence. Other personnel have heard rumors to the effect that Peters has become involved with another woman, but none of them will admit that they have any firsthand information to support the rumor. Rumors of this sort are common in your department.

        6. Peters has no record of previous disciplinary action.

  II. The problem.

    A. You are to interview Officer Peters in an attempt to protect your department (and your subordinate.) This is an initial interview.

B. What are your objectives?
C. How will you approach the interview?
   1. What further information may you want to get before the interview?
   2. What kinds of questions will you ask?
D. What other actions might you take?

A Note on Stress Training

The kind of training described is concerned with the management of stress. There is, however, another use of the term stress training. This is training based on the hypothesis that subjecting a trainee to stressful situations will increase his ability to cope with them. Usually this takes the form of authoritarian harassment and hazing (Earle, 1973), a degradation ritual similar to that which Goffman (1962) and others (Earle, 1973) describe in military boot camps. The stress pervades the training. In contrast, nonstress training emphasizes academic achievement, and the exercise of individual judgment and discretion (Earle, 1973).

Earle (1973) compared classes from the academy of the Los Angeles sheriff's department that were trained by each of these methods. He found that non-stress-trained subjects performed at a significantly higher level in the areas of field performance, job satisfaction, and performance acceptability by persons served than those with traditional stress training. Ruddock (1974) reports similar results for the Columbus, Ohio, police department. He states particularly that stress training "failed to develop self-discipline to any great extent; and it had no provisions for the recruit to make decisions for himself" (p. 47).

A variation on stress training involves specific training for response in stressful situations. This includes situational training in the use of firearms (the "shoot/don't shoot" simulations) (Slater and Lovette, 1978) and role playing in the handling of domestic disputes (Bard, 1969). Under these circumstances the recruit can clearly see the reasons for the pressure and respect their legitimacy: there is no taint of degradation by academy pesonnel. This kind of training has generally been successful in improving responses under pressure.

NOTES

1. Portions of this material appeared earlier in Katherine W. Ellison, John P. Cross, and John L. Genz, Training in Stress Management, *Police Chief, 47(9):*27 – 31, 1980.

2. These courses were developed primarily for use in the police academies of Middlesex, Essex, and Bergen Counties in New Jersey, but parts of them have been used with other agencies. More than 700 officers of all ranks took part in the courses given for these three academies. The authors wish to thank the directors of these academies, Matthew Zaleski, Henry Lyons, and Ronald Calissi for their support and encouragement. The instructors who worked with us are listed in the Acknowledgments.

3. The authors' material was based on the theory they have presented here; they now are in the arduous process of developing and carrying out what they hope will be useful follow-up evaluations; however, they still will lay no claim to have developed evaluation programs that completely satisfy purists among evaluation researchers: such work is beyond their current financial (and time) means.

4. Morton Bard's (1970) pioneering work in handling domestic disputes used graduate students extensively in the officers' training.

5. Examples of class schedules for each group will be presented later in this chapter.

6. Chapters 1 and 2 are greatly expanded versions of these lectures.

7. The fear of legal repercussions seems to be one of the greatest motivators of police administrators for programs of this sort.

8. The authors must confess, however, that Deputy Chiefs Thomas Granahan, East Orange, New Jersey Police Department, and John Cross, Newark, New Jersey Police Department, have been extremely successful as instructors in this course.

EPILOGUE

GOOD policing is not impossible. In the authors' years of association with officers, they have seen many who do their jobs with skill and understanding. In addition, the reactions that have been associated with stress are not inevitable. Many officers retire in good physical and emotional health and look back on their careers with pleasure.

The reactions associated with pressure, however, are common enough and potentially deleterious enough to personal well-being and the ability to function well on the job that they deserve consideration. Efforts at systematic study of the best techniques for dealing with pressure are relatively new, and conclusions are, at best, tentative. In writing this book the authors decided not to wait the years it might take until all the returns are in. Stress has become a fad in policing, as it has in other occupations, and many claims for cures are being promoted. In light of this the authors have tried to present the current evidence with such cautions as seemed appropriate.

Change is not easy, nor can anyone think that one change, however major, will bring everlasting happiness. Change must be constant, as social conditions in the world around us vary. If one can accept this inevitability and see it as a challenge instead of a threat, life will be easier.

Selye has said that the worst of all modern stressors is purposelessness. Despite the setbacks, every officer can remember times when he made a difference in people's lives, giving them the aid they needed to cope with a chaotic world. At their best, the police represent a force for the order necessary for society to function. It is not an easy job, but it is one that is worth doing well. This is the challenge that the authors hope will sustain officers and help them to be, as Niederhoffer (1967) puts it, "tolerant observers of the human comedy," and perhaps even dedicated and successful agents for change.

BIBLIOGRAPHY

Abram, Harry S. (Ed.). *Psychological Aspects of Stress.* Springfield: Thomas, 1970.

Akerstedt, T., and Torvall, L. Experimental changes in shift schedules: Their effects on well-being. *Ergonomics, 21(101):*849 – 856, 1978.

Aldang, Ramon J., and Brief, Arthur P. Supervisory styles and police role stress. *Journal of Police Science and Administration, 6(3):*362 – 367, 1978.

Alex, N. *Black in Blue.* New York: Appleton, 1969.

Aldwin, C. M. Commitments, coping, hassles and uplifts. Paper presented at the annual meeting of the American Psychological Association, Washington, D. C., 1982.

Antonovsky, A. Twenty-five years later: A limited study of the sequelae of the concentration camp experience. *Social Psychiatry, 6:*186 – 193, 1971.

Aries, Philippe. *Centuries of Childhood.* New York: Knopf, 1962.

Axelberd, Mark, and Valle, Jose. South Florida's approach to police stress management. *Police Stress, 1(1):*13 – 14, 1979.

Bard, Morton. *Training Police as Specialists in Family Crisis Intervention.* Washington: U. S. Government Printing Office, 1970.

Bard, Morton, and Ellison, Katherine. Crisis intervention and investigation of forcible rape. *Police Chief, 41(5):*68 – 73, 1974.

Baxter, D. Coping with police stress. *Trooper, 3(4):*68, 1978.

Bayley, David H., and Mendelsohn, M. *Minorities and the Police.* New York: Free Press, 1969.

Beck, A. T. *Cognitive Therapy and Emotional Disorders.* New York: New American Library, 1979.

Bennet, W., and Gurin, J. *The Dieter's Dilemma.* New York: Basic Books, 1981.

Bennett-Sandler, Georgette, and Ubell, Earl. Time bombs in blue. *New York Magazine,* 47 – 51, March 21, 1977.

Benson, Herbert. *The Relaxation Response.* New York: Morrow, 1975.

Benson, Herbert, and Allen, Robert L. How much stress is too much? *Harvard Business Review, 58(5):*86 – 92, 1980.

Birk, L. Cited in Meichenbaum, D. H. *Cognitive Behavior Modification: An Integrative Approach.* New York: Plenum, 1975.

Blackmore, J. Are police allowed to have problems of their own? *Police, 1(3):*47 – 55, 1978.

Borkovec, T. D., and Hennings, B. I. The role of physiological attention focusing in the relaxation treatment of sleep disturbance, general tension, and specific stress reaction. *Behavior Research and Therapy, 16:*7 – 19, 1978.

Boss, R. W. It doesn't matter if you win or lose, unless you're losing: Organizational change in a law enforcement agency. *Journal of Applied Behavioral Science,* 189 – 219, 1979.

Boswell, Philip C., and Murray, Edward J. Effects of meditation on psychological and physiological measures of anxiety. *Journal of Consulting and Clinical Psychology, 47(3):*606 – 607, 1979.

Brenner, M. H. *Mental Illness and the Economy.* Cambridge: Harvard, 1973.

Broderick, John J. *Police in a Time of Change.* Morristown: General Learning, 1977.

Brodyaga, L., Gates, M., Singer, S., Tucker, M. and White, R. *Rape and Its Victims: A Report for Citizens, Health Facilities and Criminal Justice Agencies.* Washington, D. C.: LEAA, 1975.

Broverman, I. K., Broverman, D. M., Clarkson, F. E., Rosenkrantz, P. S., and Vogel, S. R. Sex-role stereotypes and clinical judgments of mental health. *Journal of Consulting and Clinical Psychology, 28:*59 – 78, 1970.

Brown, L. P., and Martin, E. E. Neighborhood team policing: A viable concept in Multnoma County. *Police Chief,* May, 1976.

Browning, Rufus. Personal communication, 1982.

Bruner, J. Personality change. *Psychology Today,* 1978.

Brunner, George D. Law enforcement officers' work schedule reactions. *Police Chief, 43(1):*30 – 31, 1976.

Bullard, Peter D. *Coping with Stress: A Psychological Survival Manual.* Portland: ProSeminar Press, 1980.

Burke, Ronald J. Occupational stress and job satisfaction. *Journal of Social Psychology, 100:*235 – 244, 1976.

Burke, Ronald J., and Bradshaw, Patricia. Occupational and life stresses and the family. *Small Group Behavior, 12(3):*329 – 375, 1981.

Carlson, Helena M., and Sutton, Markley S. Some factors in community evaluation of police stress performance. *American Journal of Community Psychology, 7(6):*583 – 591, 1979.

Chandler, James T. The multi-department police psychologist. *Police Chief, 47(2):*34 – 36, 1980.

Cherniss, Cary. *Professional Burnout in Human Service Organizations.* New York: Praeger, 1980.

Chiriboga, David A., and Cutler, Loraine. *Stress and Adaptation: A Life Span Study.* Paper presented at Annual Convention of the American Psychological Association, New York, September 1979.

Chodoff, P., Friedman, S., and Hamburg, D. Stress, defenses, and coping behavior: Observations in parents of children with malignant disease. *American Journal of Psychiatry, 120:*743 – 749, 1964.

Coan, R. W. Personality variables associated with cigarette smoking. *Journal of Personality and Social Psychology, 26:*86 – 104, 1973.

Cobb, S. Social support as a moderator of life stress. *Psychosomatic Medicine, 38:*300 – 314, 1976.

Cofer, C. N., and Appley, M. H. *Motivation: Theory and Research.* New York: Wiley, 1964.

Cohen, Anne. I've killed that man ten thousand times. *Police, 3:*17 – 23, 1980.

Coleman, James C., Butcher, James N., and Carson, Robert C. *Abnormal Psychology and Modern Life* (6th edition). Glenview: Scott Foresman, 1980.

Collingwood, Thomas R. Police stress and physical activity. *Police Chief, 52(2):*25 – 27, 1980.

Consumers Union. Diet and heart disease. *Consumer Reports, 46(5):*256 – 260, May 1981.

Cooper, C. L., and Marshall, J. *Understanding Executive Stress.* New York: Petrocelli, 1977.

Cooper, C. L., and Marshall, J. (Eds.). *White Collar and Professional Stress.* New York: Wiley, 1980.

Cooper, C. L., and Payne, R. L. (Eds.). *Stress at Work.* New York: Wiley, 1978.

Cooper, C. L., and Payne, R. L. (Eds.). *Current Concerns in Occupational Stress.* New York: Wiley, 1980.

Cooper, K. H., Pollock, M. L., Martin, R. P., White, S. R., Linnerud, A. C., and Jackson, A. Physical fitness levels versus selected coronary risk factors. *Journal of the American Medical Association, 236:*166 – 169, 1976.

Coyne, J. C. A critique of cognitions as causal entities with particular reference to depression. *Cognitive Therapy and Research, 6*(1): 3 – 13, 1982.

Coyne, James C., and Lazarus, Richard. *The Ipsative-Normative Framework for the Longitudinal Study of Stress.* Paper presented at the Annual Convention of the American Psychological Association, New York, September 1979.

Crawford, Thomas J. Police overperception of ghetto hostility. *Journal of Police Science and Administration, 1(2):*168 – 174, 1973.

Cromwell, R. L., Butterfield, E. C., Brayfield, F. M., and Curry, J. L. *Acute Myocardial Infarction: Reaction and Recovery.* St. Louis: Mosby, 1977.

Cumming, E., Cumming, I., and Edell, L. Policeman as philosopher, guide and friend. *Social Problems, 12(3),* 1965.

Cummings, L. L., Harnett, D. L., and Stevens, O. J. Risk, fate, conciliation and trust: An international study of attitudinal differences among executives. *Academy of Management Journal, 14(3):*285 – 304, 1971.

Danto, B. L. Police suicide. *Police Stress, 1(1):*32 – 36, 40, 1978.

Dash, Jerry, and Reiser, Martin. Suicide among police in urban law enforcement agencies. *Journal of Police Science and Administration, 6:*18 – 21, 1978.

Davidson, Marilyn J., and Veno, Arthur. Police stress in Australia: A current perspective. *Australian and New Zealand Journal of Criminology, 12(3):*153 – 161, 1979.

Davidson, Marilyn J., and Veno, Arthur. Stress and the policeman. In Cooper, C. L., and Marshall, J. (Eds.). *White Collar and Professional Stress.* New York:

Wiley, 1980.

Davis, M., Eshelman, E. R., and McKay, M. *The Relaxation and Stress Reduction Workbook*. Richmond: CA: New Harbinger, 1980.

Daviss, Ben. Burnout. *Police, 5(3):*9 – 11, 14 – 18, May 1982.

DeVries, H., and Adams, G. Elecromyographic comparisons of single doses of exercise and meprobamate as to effects on muscular relaxation. *American Journal of Physical Medicine, 51:*130 – 141, 1972.

Diskin, Susan D., Goldstein, Michael J. and Grencik, Judith M. Coping patterns of law enforcement officers in simulated and naturalistic stress. *American Journal of Community Psychology, 5(1):*59 – 73, 1977.

Dohrenwend, Barbara S., and Dohrenwend, Bruce P. (Eds.). *Stressful Life Events.* New York: Wiley, 1974.

Dreifus, Claudia. A conversation with Joseph Wambaugh. *Police, 3(3):*33 – 39, 1980.

Dubos, Rene. *Man Adapting.* New Haven: Yale, 1965.

Duncan, J. T. S., Brenner, R. N., and Kravitz, M. *Police Stress: A Selected Bibliography.* Washington: U. S. Government Printing Office, 1979.

Durner, J. A., Kroeker, M. A., Miller, C. R., and Reynolds, W. R. Divorce — another occupational hazard. *Police Chief, 42(11):*48 – 53, 1975.

Earle, Howard H. *Police Recruit Training: Stress versus Non-stress.* Springfield: Thomas, 1973.

Edelwich, Jerry, and Brodsky, Archie. *Burnout: Stages of Disillusionment in the Helping Professions.* New York: Human Sciences, 1980.

Eisenberg, Terry. Job stress and the police officer: Identifying stress reduction techniques. In Kroes, William H., and Hurrell, Joseph (Eds.). *Job Stress and the Police Officer.* Washington: U. S. Government Printing Office, 1975.

Ellis, A., and Harper, R. *A New Guide to Rational Living.* North Hollywood: Wilshire, 1975.

Ellis, Albert. *Reason and Emotion in Psychotherapy.* New York: Lyle Stuart, 1962.

Ellison, Katherine W. The stress syndrome of the modern police officer. In Scanlon, Robert A. (Ed.). *Law Enforcement Bible No. 2.* South Hackensack: Stoeger, 1982.

Ellison, Katherine W., and Buckhout, Robert. *Psychology and Criminal Justice.* New York: Harper, 1981.

Ellison, Katherine W., Cross, John P., and Genz, John L. Training in stress management. *Police Chief, 47(9):*27 – 31, 1980.

Ellison, Katherine W., and Genz, John L. The police officer as burned-out samaritan. *FBI Law Enforcement Bulletin, 47(3):*1 – 7, 1978.

Engler, L. J. *Rotating vs. Permanent Shift Schedules.* Unpublished master's thesis, Rutgers University, Newark, New Jersey, 1980.

Epley, S. W. Reduction of the behavioral effects of aversive stimulation by the presence of companions. *Psychological Bulletin, 81:*271 – 283, 1974.

Erikson, Kai T. *Everything in its Path: Destruction of Community in the Buffalo Creek Flood.* New York: Simon and Schuster, 1976.

Esbeck, Edward S., and Halverson, George. Stress and tension — team building for the professional police officer. *Journal of Police Science and Administration,* *1(2):*153 – 161, 1973.

Farquhar, W., and Lowe, J. A list of irrational ideas. In Tosi, D. J. *Youth Toward Personal Growth, A Rational Emotive Approach.* Columbus: Merrill, 1974.

Fenster, C. A., and Schlossberh, H. The psychologist as police department consultant. In Platt, J. J., and Wicks, R. J. (Eds.). *The Psychological Consultant.* New York: Grune and Stratton, 1979.

Festinger, Leon. *A Theory of Cognitive Dissonance.* Stanford: Stanford, 1957.

Fiedler, Fred E. *A Theory of Effective Leadership.* New York: McGraw-Hill, 1967.

Fletcher, Ben C., and Payne, Roy L. Stress and work: A review and theoretical framework, I. *Personnel Review, 9(1):*19 – 29, 1980.

Fletcher, Ben C., and Payne, Roy L. A review and theoretical framework II. *Personnel Review, 9(2):*5 – 8, 1980.

Folkard, S., and Monk, T. H. Shiftwork and performance. *Human Factors, 21(4):*483 – 492, 1979.

Follmann, Joseph F., Jr. *Helping the Troubled Employee.* New York: AMACOM, 1978.

Foreyt, J., and Rathjen, D. (Eds.). *Cognitive Behavior Therapy: Research and Application.* New York: Plenum, 1978.

Fox, S. J., Naughton, J. P., and Haskell, W. Physical activity and the prevention of coronary heart disease. *Annals of Clinical Research, 3:*404 – 432, 1971.

Frankl, Viktor E. *Man's Search for Meaning* (revised edition). New York: Simon and Schuster, 1962.

French, John R. P. A comparative look at stress and strain in policemen. In Kroes, William H., and Hurrell, Joseph J. (Eds.). *Job Stress and the Police Officer.* Washington: U. S. Government Printing Office, 1975.

Freudenberger, Herbert J. *Burn-out: The High Cost of High Achievement.* Garden City, NY: Anchor, 1980.

Friedman, M., and Rosenman, R. Association of specific overt behavior pattern with blood and cardiovascular findings. *Journal of the American Medical Association, 169:*1286, 1959.

Friedman, M., and Rosenman, R. *Type A Behavior and Your Heart.* New York: Knopf, 1974.

Friedman, P. Suicide among police: A study of ninety-three suicides among New York policemen 1934 – 1940. In Schneidman, E. (Eds.). *Essays in Self-Destruction.* New York: Science House, 1968.

Fuchs, C. Z., and Rehm, L. P. A self-control behavior therapy program for depression. *Journal of Consulting and Clinical Psychology, 45:*206 – 215, 1977.

Garfield, S. L., and Bergin, A. E. (Eds.). *Handbook of Psychotherapy and Behavior Change* (2nd edition). New York: Wiley, 1978.

Garfield, S. L., and Kurtz, R. Clinical psychologists in the 1970's. *American Psychologist, 31:*1 – 9, 1976.

Gay, W. C., Woodward, J. P., Day, H. T., O'Neil, J. P., and Tacher, C. J. *Issues in Team Policing: A Review of the Literature.* Washington: National Sheriffs' Association, 1975.

Gergen, Kenneth J., and Gergen, Mary M. *Social Psychology*. New York: Harcourt Brace Jovanovich, 1981.

Glass, D. C. *Behavior Patterns, Stress, and Coronary Disease*. Hillsdale, NJ: Erlbaum, 1977.

Glass, D. C., Singer, J. E., and Friedman, L. N. Psychic costs of adaptation to an environmental stressor. *Journal of Personality and Social Psychology, 12:*200 – 210, 1969.

Glesner, G. C., Green, B. L., and Winget, C. N. Quantifying interview data on psychic impairment in disaster survivors. *Journal of Nervous and Mental Disease, 166:*209 – 216, 1978.

Goffman, E. *Asylums*. New York: Doubleday, 1962.

Goldberg, E. L., and Comstock, G. W. Life events and subsequent illness. *American Journal of Epidemiology, 104:*146 – 158, 1976.

Goldman, Barbara L., Domitor, Paul J., and Murray, Edward J. Effects of Zen meditation on anxiety reduction and peceptual functioning. *Journal of Consulting and Clinical Psychology, 47(3):*551 – 556, 1979.

Greenberg, Ilene, and Smith, Bradford. *Police Policies and Patrol Officer Satisfaction with Department Operations*. Washington: National Institute of Law Enforcement and Criminal Justice, 1979.

Grencik, Judith M. Toward an understanding of stress. In Kroes, William H., and Hurrell, Joseph J. (Eds.). *Job Stress and the Police Officer*. Washington: U. S. Government Printing Office, 1975.

Gross, S. Bureaucracy and decision-making: Viewed from a patrol precinct level. *Police Chief, 42(1):*59 – 64, 1975.

Guralnick, L. Morality by occupation and cause of death among men 20 – 64 years of age: United States 1950. *Vital Statistics, Special Report 53(3)*, 1963.

Hachman, R. J., Oldham, G., Janson, R., and Purdy, K. A new strategy for job enrichment. *California Management Review, 17:*57 – 71, 1975.

Hageman, Mary J. C. Occupational stress and marital relationships. *Journal of Police Science and Administration, 6(4):*402 – 412, 1978.

Hageman, Mary J. C., Kennedy, Robert B., and Price, Norman. Coping with stress. *Police Chief, 46:*27 – 28, 1979.

Hampton, D., Summer, C., and Webber, R. *Organizational Behavior and the Practice of Management*. Glenview: Scott Foresman, 1980.

Handy, C. The family: Help or hindrance? In Cooper, C. L., and Payne, R. (Eds.). *Stress at Work*. New York: Wiley, 1978.

Haynes, William D. *Stress Related Disorders in Policemen*. San Francisco: R & E Research Associates, 1978.

Heiman, M. F. Police suicide. *Journal of Police Science and Administration, 3:*267 – 271, 1975.

Heiman, M. F. Suicide among police. *American Journal of Psychiatry, 134:*1289 – 1290, 1977.

Heron, W. Cognitive and physiological effects of perceptual isolation. In Solomon, P. (Ed.). *Sensory Deprivation*. Cambridge: Harvard, 1961.

Herzberg, Frederick. One more time: How do you motivate employees? *Harvard*

Business Review, January – February 1968.

Hightshoe, N., and Hightshoe, R. The St. Louis County Department of Police Family Program. *Police Chief, 45(4):*34, 36, 95, 1978.

Hillgren, J. S., Bond, R. B., and Jones, S. Primary stressors in police administration and law enforcement. *Journal of Police Science and Administration, 4:*445 – 449, 1976.

Holmes, Thomas H., and Masuda, Minoru. Life change and illness susceptibility. In Dohrenwend, B. S., and Dohrenwend, B. P. (Eds.). *Stressful Life Events*. New York: Wiley, 1974.

Holmes, Thomas H., and Rahe, Richard H. The social readjustment rating scale. *Journal of Psychosomatic Medicine, 11:*213 – 218, 1967.

Holmes, T. S., and Holmes, T. H. Short-term intrusions into the life-style routine. *Journal of Psychosomatic Research, 14:*121 – 132, 1970.

Holroyd, Kenneth A. Stress, coping and the treatment of stress-related illness. In McNamara, J. R. (Ed.). *Behavioral Approaches in Medicine: Application and Analysis*. New York: Plenum, 1979.

Holroyd, Kenneth A., and Andrasik, Frank. Coping and the self-control of chronic tension headaches. *Journal of Consulting and Clinical Psychology, 46(5):*1036 – 1043, 1978.

Holroyd, Kenneth A., and Andrasik, Frank, and Westbrook, Teresa. Cognitive control of tension headache. *Cognitive Therapy and Research, 1(2):*121 – 133.

Holstrom, Lynda L., and Burgess, Ann W. *The Victim of Rape: Institutional Reactions*. New York: Wiley, 1978.

Hudgens, R. W. Personal catastrophe and depression: A consideration of the subject with respect to medically ill adolescents and a requiem for retrospective life events studies. In Dohrenwend, B. S., and Dohrenwend, B. P. (Eds.). *Stressful Life Events*. New York: Wiley, 1974.

Iannone, N. F. *Supervision of Police Personnel*, (3rd edition). Englewood Cliffs: Prentice-Hall, 1980.

Ikemi, Y., Nagata, S., Ago, Y., and Ikemi, A. Self-control over stress. *Journal of Psychosomatic Research, 26(1):*51 – 56, 1982.

Innes, J. M. Social psychological approaches to the study of the induction and alleviation of stress: Influences upon health and illness. In Stephenson, G. M., and Davis, J. M. (Eds.). *Progress in Applied Social Psychology, volume I*. New York: Wiley, 1981.

James, P., and Nelson, M. The police family — A wife's eye view. *FBI Law Enforcement Bulletin, 45(11):*12 – 22, 1975.

Janis, I. Psychodynamic aspects of stress tolerance. In Klausner, S. (Ed.). *The Quest for Self-Control*. New York: Free Press, 1965.

Jenkins, C. David. Psychosocial modifiers of response to stress. In Barrett, James E. et al. (Eds.). *Stress and Mental Disorder*. New York: Raven, 1979.

Johnson, J. H., and Sarason, I. G. Recent developments in research on life stress. In Hamilton, V., and Warburton, D. M. (Eds.). *Human Stress and Cognition*. Chichester, England: Wiley, 1979.

Kahn, Robert. Job burnout: Prevention and remedies. *Public Welfare*, 61 – 62,

Spring 1978.

Kaplan, M. *The Partial Transformation of a State Mental Hospital into a Comprehensive Community Mental Health Center: A Case Study of Worcester State Hospital.* Unpublished doctor of psychology professional report, University of Illinois at Champaign-Urbana, 1975.

Karger, Howard J. Burnout as alienation. *Social Science Review*, 270 – 283, 1981.

Kasl, S. V. Epidemiological contributions to the study of work stress. In Cooper, C. L., and Payne, R. L. (Eds.). *Stress at Work.* London: Wiley, 1978.

Katz, J., Weiner, H., Gallagher, T., and Hellman, L. Stress, distress and ego defenses. *Archives of General Psychiatry, 23:*131 – 142, 1970.

Kazoroski, Ron. Formulation of goals in law enforcement agencies. *Police Chief, 47:*62 – 65, 1980.

Kelling, George, and Pate, Mary Ann. The person-role fit in policing: The current knowledge. In Kroes, William H., and Hurrell, Joseph J. (Eds.). *Job Stress and the Police Officer.* Washington: U. S. Government Printing Office, 1975.

Kirkham, George L. From professor to patrolman: A fresh perspective on the police. *Journal of Police Science and Administration, 2(3):*127 – 137, 1974.

Kirkham, George L. The metamorphosis. In Kroes, William H., and Hurrell, Joseph J. (Eds.). *Job Stress and the Police Officer.* Washington: U. S. Government Printing Office, 1975.

Kobasa, S. C. Stressful life events, personality and health: An inquiry into hardiness. *Journal of Personality and Social Psychology, 37:*1 – 11, 1979.

Koriat, A., Melkman, R., Averill, J. R., and Lazarus, R. S. The self-control of emotional reactions to a stressful film. *Journal of Personality, 40:*601 – 619, 1972.

Kossen, Stan. *The Human Side of Organizations.* San Francisco: Canfield, 1975.

Kroes, William H. *Society's Victim — The Policeman.* Springfield: Thomas, 1976.

Kroes, W. H., and Gould, S. Job stress in policemen: An empirical study. *Police Stress*, 1982.

Kroes, William H., and Gould, Sam. Stress in policemen. *Police Stress, 1:*9 – 10, 1979.

Kroes, William H., Hurrell, Joseph J., and Margolis, Bruce. Job stress in police administrators. *Journal of Police Science and Administration, 2(4):*381 – 387, 1974.

Kroes, William H., Margolis, Bruce, and Hurrell, Joseph J. Job stress in policemen. *Journal of Police Science and Administration, 2:*145 – 155, 1974.

Labovitz, S., and Hagedorn, S. An analysis of suicide rates among occupational categories. *Sociological Inquiry, 41:*57 – 71, 1971.

Lakein, A. *How to Get Control of Your Time and Your Life.* New York: Signet, 1973.

Langer, E. J., Janis, I. L., and Wolfer, J. A. Reduction of psychological stress in surgical patients. *Journal of Experimental Social Psychology, 11:*155 – 165, 1975.

LaRocca, James M., and Jones, Allan P. Co-worker and leader support as moderators of stress-strain relationships in work situations. Report Number 77 – 51, submitted by Naval Medical Research and Development Command, Department of the Navy (undated).

Lawrence, Richard Allen. *The Measurement and Prediction of Police Job Stress.* Doctoral dissertation, Sam Houston State University, Huntsville, TX, 1978.

Lazarus, A. A. *Behavior Therapy and Beyond.* New York: McGraw-Hill, 1971.

Lazarus, Richard S. *Psychological Stress and the Coping Process.* New York: McGraw-Hill, 1966.

Lazarus, Richard S. The concept of stress and disease. In Levi, L. (Ed.). *Society, Stress and Disease, volume 1.* London: Oxford, 1971.

Lazarus, Richard S. Positive denial: The case for not facing reality. *Psychology Today, 13(6):*44 – 60, 1979.

Lefcourt, H. M. *Locus of Control: Current Trends in Theory and Research.* Hillside, NJ: Erlbaum, 1976.

Lefkowitz, Joel. Industrial-organizational psychology and the police. *American Psychologist, 32(5):*346 – 364, 1977.

Lerner, M. J., and Miller, D. T. Just world research and the attribution process. *Psychological Bulletin, 85:*1030 – 1051, 1978.

Lester, David. Occupational injuries, illness and fatalities in police officers. *Police Chief, 48:*43, 1981.

Levi, Lennart. Psychosocial factors in preventive medicine. In National Academy of Sciences (Ed.). *Healthy People: The Surgeon General's Report on Health Promotion and Disease Prevention, Background Papers.* Washington: U. S. Government Printing Office, 1979.

Levy, R. J. Predicting police failures. *Journal of Criminal Law, Criminology and Police Science, 58:*265 – 275, 1967.

Lewis, R. Toward an understanding of police anomie. *Journal of Police Science and Administration, 1:*484 – 490, 1973.

Leyden, J. P. Police stress: A possible approach. *FBI Law Enforcement Bulletin, 46:*25 – 29, 1977.

Lifton, Robert J. *Death in Life: Survivors of Hiroshima.* New York: Random House, 1968.

Lifton, R. J., and Olson, E. The human meaning of total disaster. *Psychiatry, 39:*1 – 18, 1976.

Linscott, Judy. On-the-job fitness may be the shape of things to come. *New York Daily News,* July 21, 1981.

Locke, E. A. The nature and causes of job satisfaction. In Dunnette, M. D. (Ed.). *Handbook of Industrial and Organizational Psychology.* Chicago: Rand McNally, 1976.

Lumsden, D. P. Towards a systems model of stress: Feedback from an anthropological study of the impact of Ghana's Volta River project. In Sarason, I. G., and Spielberger, C. D. (Eds.). *Stress and Anxiety, volume 2.* Washington: Hemisphere, 1975.

Lynn, S. J., and Freedman, R. R. Transfer and evaluation of biofeedback treatment. In Goldstein, A. P., and Kanfer, F. (Eds.). *Maximizing Treatment Gains: Transfer Enhancement in Psychotherapy.* New York: Academic, 1979.

McKay, M., Davis, M., and Fanning, P. *Thoughts and Feelings: The Art of Cognitive Stress Intervention.* Richmond, CA: New Harbinger, 1981.

McKenna, Jack F., Oritt, Paul L., and Wolff, Howard K. Occupational stress as a predictor in the turnover decision. *Journal of Human Stress*, 12 – 17, December 1981.

Mahoney, M., and Arkoff, D. Cognitive and self-control therapies. In Garfield, S., and Bergin, A. (Eds.). *Handbook of Psychotherapy and Behavior Change: An Empirical Analysis*. New York: Wiley, 1978.

Margolies, B., Kroes, W. H., and Quinn, R. Job stress: An unlisted occupational hazard. *Journal of Occupational Medicine, 16(10)*:659 – 661, 1974.

Maris, L., and Maris, M. The mechanics of stress release: The Transcendental Meditation program and occupational stress. *Police Work*, 48 – 56, April 1978.

Martin, Susan E. *Breaking and Entering: Policewomen in the Police World*. Unpublished doctoral dissertation, Washington, D. C., George Washington University, 1977.

Martin, Susan E. *Police*women and police*women* — occupational role dilemmas and choices of female officers. *Journal of Police Science and Administration, 7(3)*:314 – 323, 1979.

Martin, Susan E. *Breaking and Entering*. Berkeley: California, 1980.

Maslach, Christina. Burned out. *Human Behavior, 1*:16 – 22, 1976.

Maslach, Christina. *Burnout — The Cost of Caring*. Englewood Cliffs: Prentice-Hall, 1982.

Maslach, Christina, and Jackson, Susan E. Burned-out cops and their families. *Psychology Today, 12(12)*:59 – 62, 1979.

Mason, J. W., Maher, J. T., Hartley, L. H., Mougey, E., Perlow, M. J., and Jones, L. G. Selectivity of corticosteroid and catecholamine responses to natural stimuli. In Serban, G. (Ed.). *Psychopathology of Human Adaptation*. New York: Plenum, 1976.

Matteson, M. T., and Ivancevich, J. M. Organizational stressors and heart disease: A research model. *The Academy of Management Review, 4*:213 – 222, 1979.

Matthews, K. A., Scheier, M. F., Brunson, B. I., and Carducci, B. *Why Do Unpredictable Events Lead to Reports of Physical Symptoms?* Paper presented at the meeting of the American Psychological Association, New York, 1979.

Maynard, Peter E., and Maynard, Nancy W. Preventing police family stress through couples communication training. *Police Chief, 47(2)*:30 – 31, 66, 1980.

Maynard, Peter E., Maynard, Nancy W., McCubbin, Hamilton I., and Shao, David. Family life and the police profession: Coping patterns wives employ in managing job stress and the family environment. *Family Relations, 29*:495 – 501, 1980.

Mechanic, David. *Students Under Stress*. New York: Free Press, 1962.

Meers, A., Maasen, A., and Verhaagen, P. Subjective health after six months and after four years of shift work. *Ergonomics, 21(10)*:857 – 859, 1978.

Megerson, J. The officer's lady: A followup. *Police Chief, 43*(1):50 – 52, 1976.

Meichenbaum, Donald H. Toward a cognitive theory of self-control. In Garfield, S. L., and Bergin, A. E. (Eds.). *Consciousness and Self-Regulation: Advances in Re-*

search, volume 1. New York: Plenum, 1975.

Meichenbaum, Donald H. *Cognitive Behavior Modification: An Integrative Approach*. New York: Plenum, 1977.

Meichenbaum, D., Turk, D., and Burstein, S. The nature of coping with stress. In Sarason, I. G., and Spielberger, C. D. (Eds.). *Stress and Anxiety*, volume 2. Washington: Hemisphere, 1975.

Mills, Robert B. Simulated stress in police recruit selection. In Kroes, William H., and Hurrell, Joseph J. (Eds.). *Job Stress and the Police Officer*. Washington: U. S. Government Printing Office, 1975.

Mischel, Walter, and Mischel, Harriet Nerlove. *Essentials of Psychology*. New York: Random House, 1977.

Monat, A., and Lazarus, R. S. (Eds.). *Stress and Coping*. New York: Columbia, 1977.

More, Harry W. *Effective Police Administration: A Behavioral Approach*. San Jose: Justice Systems Development, 1975.

Morris, J. N., Chaves, P. N., Adam, C., Sirey, C., and Epstein, L. Vigorous exercise in leisure-time and the incidence of coronary heart disease. *Lancet, 1:*333 – 339, 1973.

Morrow, L. The burnout of almost everyone. *Time*, September 21, 1981.

Mott, Paul E., Mann, Floyd C., McLoughlin, Quin, and Warwick, Donald P. *Shift Work*. Ann Arbor: University of Michigan Press, 1965.

Naditch, M. P. Locus of control, relative discontent and hypertension. *Social Psychiatry, 9:*111 – 117, 1974.

Naditch, M. P., Gargan, M., and Michael, L. B. Denial, anxiety, locus of control and the discrepancy between aspirations and achievements as components of depression. *Journal of Abnormal Psychology, 84:*1 – 9, 1975.

Naughton, R. J. Motivational factors of American prisoners of war in Vietnam. *Naval War College Review, 27(4):*2 – 14, 1975.

Nelson, Z. P., and Smith, W. The law enforcement profession: An incidence of high suicide. *Omega, 1:*293 – 299, 1970.

Niederhoffer, Arthur. *Behind the Shield*. Garden City: Doubleday, 1967.

Niederhoffer, Arthur, and Niederhoffer, Elaine. *The Police Family: From Station House to Ranch House*. Lexington: Lexington, 1978.

Norfolk, D. *The Stress Factor*. New York: Simon & Schuster, 1977.

Novaco, Raymond. *Anger Control: The Development and Evaluation of an Experimental Treatment*. Lexington: Heath, 1975.

Novaco, Raymond. A stress-inoculation approach to anger management in the training of law enforcement officers. *American Journal of Community Psychology, 5(3):*327 – 346, 1977.

Obrist, P. The cardiovascular-behavioral interaction — as it appears today. *Psychophysiology, 13:*95 – 107, 1976.

Ouchi, William G. *Theory Z: How American Business Can Meet the Japanese Challenge*. Reding, MS: Addison-Wesley, 1981.

Pendergrass, Virginia E., and Ostrove, Nancy M. *Survey of Stress in Women in Policing*. Paper presented at the annual convention of the American Psychological

Association, Washington, D. C., August 25, 1982.

Peter, Lawrence. *The Peter Principle*. New York: Bantam, 1969.

Phillips, E., and Cheston, R. Conflict resolution: What works? *California Management Review, 21*(4):76 – 83, 1979.

Pines, A. Helper's motivation and the burnout syndrome. In Wills, T. A. (Ed.) *Basic Processes in Helping Relationships*. New York: Academic, 1982.

Pines, A., and Maslach, C. Characteristics of staff burnout in mental health settings. *Hospital and Community Psychiatry, 29*:233 – 237, 1978.

Powlege, F. The therapist as double agent. *Psychology Today, 10*(7):44 – 47, 1977.

Price, C. S., Pollock, M. L., Gettman, L. R., and Dent, D. A. *Physical Fitness Programs for Law Enforcement Officers: A Manual for Police Administrators*. Washington: U. S. Government Printing Office, 1978.

Prunier, Carol T. How is a wife supposed to compete? *Police, 2*:55 – 56, 1979.

Rabkin, Judith G., and Struening, Elmer L. Life events, stress and illness. *Science, 194*:1013 – 1020, 1976.

Rachman, S. *Fear and Courage*. San Francisco: Freeman, 1978.

Radelet, Louis A. *The Police and the Community*. Beverly Hills: Glencoe, 1980.

Reese, James T. Life in the high-speed lane: Managing police burnout. *Police Chief, 49*(6):49 – 53, 1982.

Reiser, Martin. *The Police Department Psychologist*. Springfield: Thomas, 1972.

Reiser, Martin. Some organizational stresses on policemen. *Journal of Police Science and Administration, 2*:154 – 159, 1974.

Reiser, Martin. *Practical Psychology for Police Officers*. Springfield: Thomas, 1973.

Rhead, C., Abrams, A., Trasman, H., and Margolis, P. The psychological assessment of police candidates. *American Journal of Psychiatry, 124*: 1575 – 1580, 1968.

Richard, Wayne C., and Fell, Ronald. Health factors in police job stress. In Kroes, William H., and Hurrell, Joseph J. (Eds.). *Job Stress and the Police Officer*. Washington: U. S. Government Printing Office, 1975.

Rimm, D. C., and Masters, C. *Behavior Therapy: Techniques and Empirical Findings*. New York: Academic, 1974.

Roberg, Roy. *Police Management and Organizational Behavior: A Contingency Approach*. St. Paul: West, 1979.

Rotter, Julian. Generalized expectancies for internal versus external control of reinforcement. *Psychological Monographs, 80*:1, 1966.

Ruddock, Robert L. Recruit training: Stress v. nonstress. *Police Chief, 42*(11):47 – 50, 1974.

Ryan, William. *Blaming the Victim*. New York: Vintage, 1971.

Saper, M. B. Police wives: The hidden resource. *Police Chief, 47*:28 – 29, 1980.

Sarason, I. G. The revised Life Experience Survey. Unpublished manuscript, 1981. Quoted in Smith, R. E., Sarason, I. G., and Sarason, B. R. *Psychology: The Frontiers of Behavior* (2nd edition). New York: Harper, 1982.

Sarason, I. G., Johnson, J. H., and Siegel, J. M. Assessing the impact of life stress: Development of the Life Experience Survey. *Journal of Consulting and Clinical Psychology, 46*:932 – 946, 1978.

Schachter, Stanley. Don't sell habit-breakers short. *Psychology Today, 16(8):*27 – 33, 1982.

Schramm, Carl J., Mandell, Wallace, and Archer, Janet. *Workers Who Drink: Their Treatment in an Industrial Setting.* Washington: U.S. Dept. of Labor, 1979.

Seer, Peter. Psychological control of essential hypertension: Review of the literature and methodological critique. *Psychological Bulletin, 86(6):*1015 – 1043, 1979.

Seer, Peter, and Raeburn, John M. Meditation training and essential hypertension: A methodological study. *Journal of Behavioral Medicine, 3(1):*59 – 71, 1980.

Seligman, M. E. P. *Helplessness.* San Francisco: Freeman, 1975.

Selye, Hans. *The Stress of Life.* New York: McGraw-Hill, 1952.

Selye, Hans (Interviewed by Laurence Cherry.). On the real benefits of eustress. *Psychology Today, 12:*60 – 63, 69 – 70, 1978.

Selye, Hans. The stress of police work. *Police Stress, 1(1):* 1978.

Sewell, James D. Police stress. *FBI Law Enforcement Bulletin, 50(4):*7 – 11, 1981.

Shaffer, Martin. *Life After Stress.* New York: Plenum, 1982.

Shapiro, D. H., and Zifferblatt, S. M. Zen meditation and behavioral self-control: Similarities, differences, and clinical applications. *American Psychologist, 31:*519 – 532, 1976.

Shaw, B. F. Comparison of cognitive therapy and behavior therapy in the treatment of depression. *Journal of Consulting and Clinical Psychology, 45:*543 – 551, 1977.

Shev, Edward E., and Hewes, Jeremy J. *Good Cops/Bad Cops: Memoirs of a Police Psychiatrist.* San Francisco: San Francisco, 1977.

Silbert, Mimi H. Job stress and burnout of new police officers. *Police Chief, 49(6):*46 – 48, 1982.

Silver, Roxane L., and Wortman, Camille B. Coping with undesirable life events. In Garber, J., and Seligman, M. E. P. (Eds.). *Human Helplessness.* New York: Academic, 1980.

Singleton, Gary W., and Teahan, John. Effects of job-related stress on the physical and psychological adjustment of police officers. *Journal of Police Science and Administration, 6(3):*355 – 361, 1978.

Skolnick, Jerome H. *Justice Without Trial: Law Enforcement in Democratic Society.* New York: Wiley, 1966.

Slater, Stephen L., and Lovette, Ed. Firearms stress training: Lessons learned. *Police Chief, 45(7):*51, 1978.

Smith, David. Personal communication, 1982.

Smith, J. C. Psychotherapeutic effects of transcendental meditation with control for expectation of relief and daily sitting. *Journal of Consulting and Clinical Psychology, 41:*630 – 637, 1976.

Smith, R. E., Sarason, I. G., and Sarason, B. R. *Psychology: The Frontiers of Behavior* (2nd edition). New York: Harper, 1982.

Somodevilla, S. A., Baker, C. J., Hill, W. R., and Thomas, N. H. Stress management in the Dallas Police Department. Unpublished manuscript,

1978. Quoted in Terry, W. Clinton. Police stress: The empirical evidence. *Journal of Police Science and Administration, 9(1):*61 – 75, 1981.

Spielberger, Charles D. *Police Selection and Evaluation.* New York: Praeger, 1979.

Staub, E., Tursky, B., and Schwartz, G. E. Self-control and predictability: Their effects on reactions to aversive stimulation. *Journal of Personality and Social Psychology, 18:*157 – 162, 1971.

Steinmetz, Lawrence, L. *Managing the Marginal and Unsatisfactory Performer.* Reading: Addison-Wesley, 1969.

Stewart, James K. Effective criminal investigation. *Police Chief, 47:*71 – 76, 1980.

Stotland, Ezra. Self-esteem and stress in police work. In Kroes, William H., and Hurrell, Joseph J. (Eds.). *Job Stress and the Police Officer.* Washington: U. S. Government Printing Office, 1975.

Strassberg, D. S. Relationships among locus of control, anxiety and valued goal expectations. *Journal of Consulting and Clinical Psychology, 2:*319 – 328, 1973.

Stratton, John B. Police stress, Part 1: An overview. *Police Chief, 45(5):*58 – 62, 1978.

Stratton, John B. Police stress, Part 2: Considerations and suggestions. *Police Chief, 45(5):*73 – 78, 1978.

Stratton, John B. Psychological services for police. *Journal of Police Science and Administration, 8(1):*31 – 39, 1980.

Strickland, B. R. *Locus of Control and Health Related Behaviors.* Paper presented at Inter-American Congress of Psychology, Bogota, Colombia, December 1974.

Strickland, B. R. Internal-external control of reinforcement. In Blass, T. (Ed.). *Personality Variables in Social Behavior.* Hillside, NJ: Erlbaum, 1977.

Stroebel, Charles R. *QR — The Quieting Reflex.* New York: Plenum, 1982.

Susser, Mervyn. The epidemiology of life stress. *Psychological Medicine, 11:*1 – 8, 1981. (editorial)

Sutherland, S. S., and Scherl, D. Patterns of response among rape victims. *American Journal of Orthopsychiatry, 40:*504, 1970.

Symonds, Martin. Emotional hazards of police work. *American Journal of Psychoanalysis, 30(2):*155 – 160, 1969.

Szasz, Thomas S. The psychiatrist as double agent. *Trans-action, 4:*16 – 25, 1967.

Taylor, F. G., and Marshall, W. L. Experimentl analysis of a cognitive-behavioral therapy for depression. *Cognitive Therapy and Research, 1:*59 – 72, 1978.

Teahan, John. A longitudinal study of attitudes among black and white officers. *Social Issues, 31(1):*47 – 56, 1975.

Territo, Leonard, and Vetter, Harold J. *Stress and Police Personnel.* Boston: Allyn and Bacon, 1981.

Terry, W. Clinton, III. Police stress: The empirical evidence. *Journal of Police Science and Administration, 9(1):*61 – 75, 1981.

Teten, H. D., and Sneiderman, J. W. Police personal problems: Practical considerations for administration. *FBI Law Enforcement Bulletin, 46:*8 – 15, 1977.

Thorpe, G. L., Amatu, H. I., Blakey, R. S., and Burns, J. E. Contributions of overt instructional rehearsal and "specific insight" to the effectiveness of self-instructional training: A preliminary study. *Behavior Therapy*, 7:504 – 518, 1976.

Titchener, J. L., and Kapp, F. T. Family and character change at Buffalo Creek. *American Journal of Psychiatry*, 133:295 – 299, 1976.

Toch, Hans. Quality control in police work. *Police*, 16:43 – 44, 1971.

Toch, Hans. Police morale: Living with discontent. *Journal of Police Science and Administration*, 6(3):249 – 252, 1978.

Toch, H., Grant, J. D., and Galvin, R. T. *Agents of Change: A Study of Police Reform*. New York: Wiley, 1975.

Tororiello, T. R., and Blatt, S. J. Client service implications for organizational change. *Police Chief*, 41(11):34 – 39, 1974.

Townsend, Peter. *The Family Life of Old People: An Inquiry in East London*. London: Routledge and Kegan Paul, 1957.

Trojanowicz, Robert C. *The Environment of the First-Line Police Supervisor*. Englewood Cliffs: Prentice-Hall, 1980.

Unkovic, Charles M., and Brown, William R. The drunken cop. *Police Chief*, 47:18 – 20, 1978.

van Dijkhuizen, N. *From Stressors to Strains: Research Into Their Interrelationships*. Lisse, Holland: Swets, 1980.

Walker, T. G. Behavior of temporary members in small groups. *Journal of Applied Psychology*, 58:144 – 146, 1973.

Wallace, L. Stress and its impact on the law enforcement officer. *Campus Law Enforcement Journal*, 8(4):36 – 40, 1978.

Walsh, James Leo. Career styles and police behavior. In Bayley, David H. (Ed.). *Police and Society*. Beverly Hills: Sage, 1977.

Wambaugh, Joseph. *The Onion Field*. New York: Dell, 1973.

Wambaugh, Joseph. *The Choirboys*. New York: Dell, 1975.

Wambaugh, Joseph. A conversation with Joseph Wambaugh. Interview by Dreifus, C., *Police*, 3(3):33 – 39, 1980.

Ward, Gary E. Physiological, psychological and social issues specifically related to the police profession. *Law and Order*, 27(1):12, 1979.

Watson, N. A., and Sterling, J. W. Police and Their Opinions. Gaithersburg: IACP, 1969.

Weidner, G., and Matthews, K. A. Reported physical symptoms elicited by unpredictable events and the type A coronary-prone behavior pattern. *Journal of Personality and Social Psychology*, 36:1213 – 1220, 1978.

Weil, R. J. Psychiatric aspects of disaster. In Arieti, S. (Ed.). *The World Biennial of Psychiatry and Psychotherapy, volume 2*. New York: Basic Books, 1973.

Weiss, J. M. Effects of coping behavior in different warning signal conditions on stress pathology in rats. *Journal of Comparative and Physiological Psychology*, 77:1 – 13, 1971.

Westley, William A. The escalation of violence through legitimation. *Annals*, March 1966.

White, R. W. Strategies of adaptation: An attempt at systematic description. In Coelho, G. V., Hamburg, D. A., and Adams, J. E. (Eds.). *Coping and Adapta-*

tion. New York: Basic Books, 1974.

Whitehouse, Jack E. A preliminary inquiry into the occupational disadvantages of law enforcement. *Police*, May – June, 1965.

Wilson, James Q. *Varieties of Police Behavior: The Management of Law and Order in Eight Communities.* Cambridge: Harvard, 1968.

Wisenand, Paul M. *Police Supervision: Theory and Practice* (2nd edition). Englewood Cliffs: Prentice-Hall, 1976.

Wolff, Harold G. *Stress and Disease* (2nd edition). Revised and edited by Stewart Wolf and Helen Goodell. Springfield: Thomas, 1968.

Wolpe, J. *Psychotherapy by Reciprocal Inhibition.* Stanford: Stanford University Press, 1958.

Wolpe, J. *The Practice of Behavior Therapy.* Oxford: Pergamon, 1969.

Woolfolk, Robert I, and Richardson, Frank C. *Stress, Sanity, and Survival.* New York: Monarch, 1978.

Young, R., and Ismail, A. Personality differences of adult men before and after a physical examination program. *Research Quarterly, 47(3):*513 – 519, 1976.

Zaleznik, Abraham, Kets de Vries, Manfred F. R., and Howard, John. Stress reactions in organizations: Syndromes, causes and consequences. *Behavioral Science, 22:*151 – 162, 1977.

Zimbardo, P. G. A Pirandellian prison. *New York Times Sunday Magazine*, 38 – 60, April 8, 1973.

NAME INDEX

SUBJECT INDEX